Windhover

a person... a place... a dream

Windhover Performing Arts Center
257 Granite Street (Rt. 127)
Rockport, MA 01966

www.windhover.org

First published in the United States of America by:
Twinlights Publishers, Inc.
10 Hale Street
Rockport, MA 01966
(978) 546-7398
Fax (978) 546-5803

ISBN 1-885435-14-2

10 9 8 7 6 5 4 3 2 1

Book Design by: SYP Design & Production
www.sypdesign.com

Cover Image by: Richard Winik

Printed in China

CONTENTS

The art of dancing stands at the source of all the arts that express themselves first in the human person...Dancing is the loftiest, the most moving, the most beautiful of the arts because it is no mere translation or abstraction from life; it is life itself.

—Havelock Ellis
The Dance of Life

Dance has been my life-line, literally. It has enabled me to survive unbelievable loss and given me the will to go on. In practicing dance, I have learned to see and hear with more clarity, to express ideas more powerfully, to live life itself more intensely. And all this with the simplest of means: no equipment, no fancy clothing, no conference rooms, no executive suites. To dance one needs only the presence of a body and a passion—like love.

Dance has been the through-line for Windhover as well. Without the art of dance, Windhover would never have even been conceived, and all that it has brought about would never have occurred. In a strange way, dance has enabled us both—Windhover and me—to become involved with our community through means otherwise impossible, expressing community concerns through theatrical events and collaborations. Together we have been able to discover and explore the connections between all the arts and, finally, we have been able to celebrate a place, beautiful Cape Ann, which abounds in woods, quarries, ocean, harbors, granite ledges, coves, sea birds, whales, fish, gardens, history, unique houses and people—the list goes on...

We have danced a duet together, this place and I, because, over thirty-two years, my life became as connected to Windhover's as the spirit is to the flesh. I could not separate us.

This is why I have refused to sell this one-of-a-kind place, though that would have been the easier path, as there has always been a financial struggle to keep Windhover afloat. Indeed, financial struggle has been a way of life. But I knew that if I sold Windhover, I would forever be looking again for a place just like it, and would never find one.

This book is about a place and a community, its artists, past and present, how it transforms people, how it has a life of its own and a will that is determined to go on despite difficulties. So, why write about it? To encourage anyone who has similar inclinations to follow them. To whom is this book addressed? To my grandchildren, and all the world's children and grandchildren, our future artists.

The bird hovering in the wind soars.
We, too, can soar in our imaginations.
We don't have to travel far.
We can find in the ordinary all that is extraordinary.

December, 1999

Whatever you can do
Or dream you can do,
Begin it.

Boldness has genius,
Power and magic in it.
Begin it now.

—Goethe

For a person who'd lived most of her life in a dancer's world, the purchase of a farm was a strange experience. "But I don't know how to farm," I protested when I could see that my husband was set on buying it. "Don't worry," he assured me, "I'll build you a dance center." And within six months, all during that snow-filled winter of 1967-68, he transformed every building of a farm into a dancer's world.

And yet this world is as rooted in the physical place as one could imagine. There are lawns to mow, leaves to rake, buildings to maintain. Wood tends to rot, pipes can burst, wires short circuit. But then arrives a summer night, smooth and thick as velvet, and you gaze across the garden to the outdoor stage and see what appear to be angels, dancing under the canopy of a starlit sky.

The main barn with kitchen and dining below and a dance studio above

The outdoor stage flanked by Spring and Winter statues

Section One

THE EARLY YEARS

CHAPTER 1

A Dancer's Dream

O body swayed to music, O brightening glance,
How can we know the dancer from the dance?
—*Yeats*

I was fortunate to have a very wise mother who was ahead of her time with regard to training and educating a daughter who seemed to be afflicted with an insatiable appetite for movement. Evidently I couldn't, or wouldn't, sit still, or even stay put, but she was too smart to punish me. Instead, she turned my hyperactivity into a plus by enrolling me at age three-and-a-half in Rose Sidmund's dancing classes—all of them.

Changing every hour from ballet slippers to point shoes or from tap shoes to bare feet, we were kept busy each afternoon of the week and all day Saturday when my favorite classes were scheduled—acrobatics and partnering, or what was then called "Adagio," where young men twirled and spun you around, and lifted, or even threw, you into the air with abandon. I loved the excitement, the danger, the immersion of the entire body in the intoxicating substance of motion, space, time and gravity. You knew you might be small and powerless in that other world, but here, where it really counted, in your own body, you had power.

This early experience taught me to trust myself, and to take risks—lessons that were to serve me throughout my life. I literally danced my way through middle and high school, finding every possible excuse to create and perform dances for assemblies, classes, and holiday celebrations. The only class I almost flunked was sewing. It took me the entire year to finish basting a hem. Desperate, because I never wanted to repeat that class, I created a dance and skit in which I poked fun at my failings as a seamstress. The class was in "stitches." And the teacher? Well, she passed me, if only to get rid of me!

WELLESLEY

In college, I spent four years honing my skills in critical thinking; writing hundreds of papers on the creative work of others; learning to listen, to dissect, and to evaluate. I spent many hours petitioning for a dance major, or at least for dance to be taken "seriously." Dance was considered "too specialized" to be part of the curriculum and was not academic enough to be offered except as part of the physical education program. At the time I was disappointed, but looking back I see how right Wellesley's policy was, how its emphasis on a general education opened up doors to a cultural heritage I would never have found on my own, and how it enriched my life immeasurably, both as an artist and as a "humanist." Furthermore, I received the foundation and the critical tools with which to shape my life—not a small gift!

Because dance was not part of the regular curriculum, I was forced to be resourceful in order to pursue my passion. Several of us formed a dance club and performed and created dances for every occasion we could think of—from the annual tree day pageant to dancing around the pool in Euripides' "Frogs."

I was able to dance my way through college thanks to that club, summers at Jacob's Pillow, and Wellesley's proximity to Boston, where one of the leading male dancers in the world taught a weekly class in modern dance. His name was José Limón; his assistant and leading dancer was Betty Jones. They were to have a profound and lasting effect on my life as a dancer, both as performing artists, and as teachers of a technique I have used and taught for over forty years. Some of the greatest works in the modern dance repertoire have been choreographed by Limón and by the artistic advisor to his company at that time, Doris Humphrey. So, rather than leave Wellesley because it did not offer credit for dance, I stuck it out and graduated in 1950 with honors in English Literature. I have never regretted that decision.

Ina Hahn at three-and-a-half years warming-up for performance at local movie theater

CHAPTER 2

Herb Hahn: A Man For All Seasons

Boldness has genius, power and magic in it...

He was a lieutenant in the air force, stationed at Bedford Air Force Base awaiting discharge when he came to see a dance performance at Wellesley. I was told months later that he turned to his friend and said, pointing at me, "That's the girl I'm going to marry."

Less than a year later, during my Junior year at college, his words became fact: we were married during the Christmas break. Herb was like that. His life, short as it ultimately turned out to be, was full of action, as if there were no time to waste. And there wasn't. He graduated Harvard six months early so they could send him to the air force to become a meteorologist, then off to Greenland where he monitored German planes flying over the English Channel.

Unlike everyone else stationed at the foot of the ice cap, he loved it: skiing in the summer, fishing salmon from polar streams, kayaking past glaciers to Eskimo villages, and discovering a people for whom he would have an enduring respect and love. He even learned their language—not an easy task, as there were few grammar books or dictionaries. When his tour of duty was over he volunteered to stay another year—a decision none of his GI buddies understood!

Herb was a skier when skiing was not as accessible or popular as it is today. He'd learned to ski when trails were barely groomed and when climbing up snow-laden trails with skis on your back was as natural as waiting in long lift-lines is today. In Greenland, he became a formidable skier; the Ice Cap is as hard and dangerous as it gets!

Herb Hahn Relaxing near the Ice Cap
(opposite) With two Eskimo friends

13

Air Force Lieutenant Herbert Hahn in Greenland

Herb's sailing skills were equally impressive. In all the nine or ten years we owned the "Anawan," our 42-foot bug-eye ketch, we rarely had a crew, yet he sailed it alone up and down the Northeast coast regardless of the weather—often to my dismay!

Equal in intensity to this daring physicality, was his passion for music and literature. A graduate cum laude of Harvard, he returned after the war to get his MA in English and became involved with major research on Joyce's *Finnegan's Wake*. His verbal memory was legendary—he could literally quote pages of novels and entire poems after only one reading. His teaching skills were equally notable. Over the years, dozens of his former students from Manchester High, where he headed the English department for fifteen years until his death in 1975, have told me that he was the best teacher they ever had.

These students speak of his major and enduring influence, how he made literature so immediate, accessible, and exciting! They didn't merely read Moby Dick, they went out on a whaling boat; they didn't just read Thoreau, they made a pilgrimage to Walden. They even enacted a trial for Dostoyevsky's hero of *Crime and Punishment*.

But the story I like best is: It's their first day and the students are puzzled. Where is the teacher? The bell has rung and everyone's waiting for the class to begin. Suddenly over the heads of the entire class an object flies and hits the blackboard. "'To throw' is a verb," booms a voice and they turn around in shock to see a large man who looks more like a football player than an English teacher. "I'm Mr. Hahn, your teacher. Let's get down to work." That's who he was—a man of words and action. Martha Graham said, "To dance is a verb." For Herb, living was a verb.

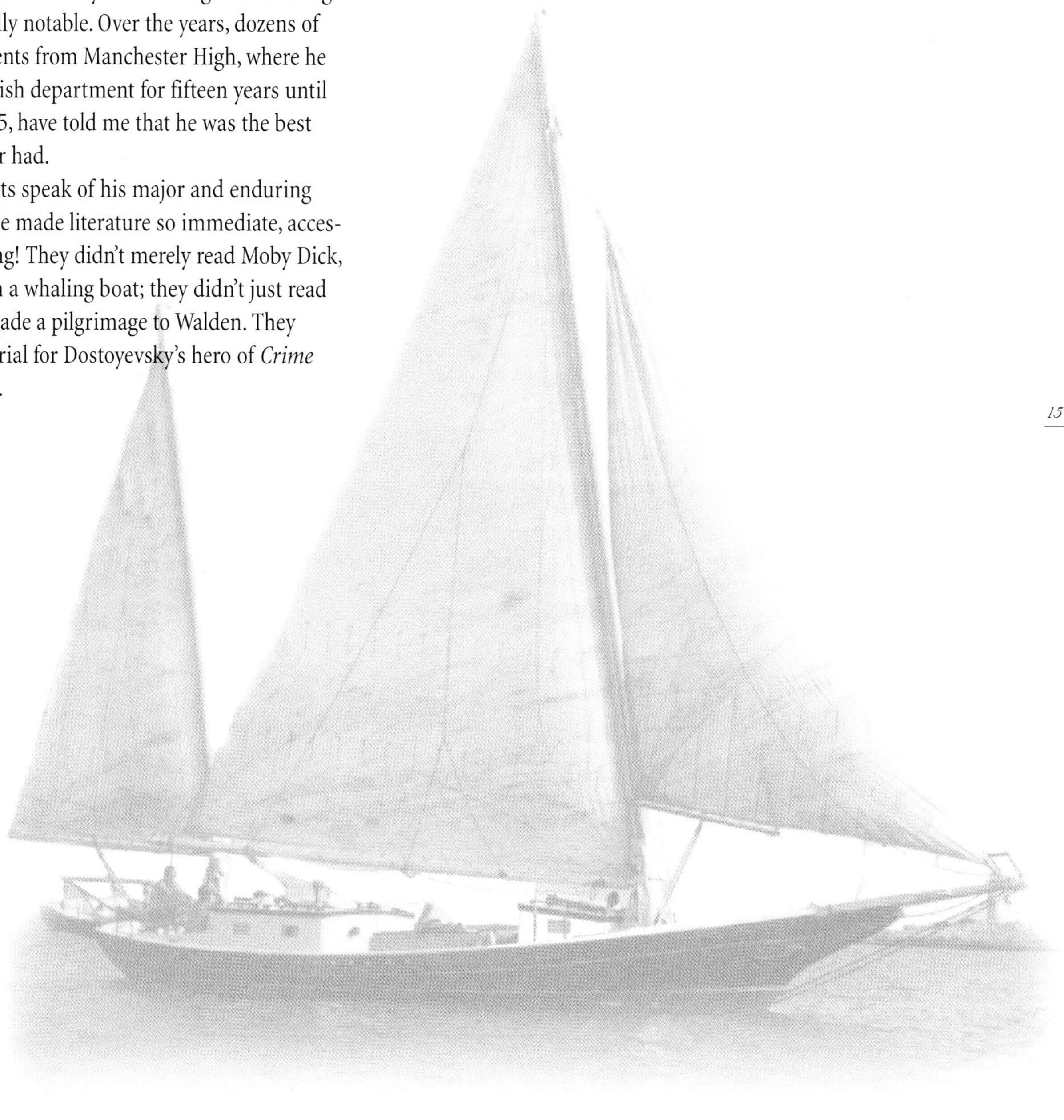

C H A P T E R 3

Academia (1946–1950)

To be master of one's body, to find a perfect union between the inner thought and outer form, to draw from this a radiance and power that makes life a more glorious and vital experience…this is to dance.

—*Doris Humphrey*

The year following my graduation from Wellesley, I accepted the position of teaching dance at Radcliffe College. I was to head a department of one person—myself. In addition to teaching, I would have the use of Sanders Theater for dance group performances and live accompaniment by the Harvard Glee Club and the Harvard Orchestra, if I so wished. I did. I spent a wonderful year teaching students my own age (I insisted they call me Ms. Hahn) and choreographing to my heart's content, using stories from the bible or from Greek myth.

That next summer, the summer of 1951, I attended The American Dance Festival at Connecticut College. José Limón, with whom I'd studied in Boston and whose work I loved, was on the faculty, as was Charles Weidman. Martha Graham's technique was taught by members of her company, and an artist who would have the greatest influence on my art and life, but whom I had barely heard of until that summer: Doris Humphrey.

I see Doris entering the large studio at Connecticut College. She walks slowly and with a cane—this once beautiful dancer who was stricken in her prime with arthritis. She speaks to us in gentle, soft tones about the dance we are going to learn. She talks about the musical structure, then has us listen over and over. It is Bach's *Passacaglia and Fugue in C Major,* choreographed in 1938, which she is reconstructing for performance at the American Dance Festival. As we learn the dance, it becomes more and more wondrous to see how she has shaped it into an architecture as strong and structurally complete as Bach's. I learn that because there is such a structure we are freed to attend to all the nuances of the dance. Much the way the skeleton supports the body, Doris' structure supports our movements.

Doris said of "Passacaglia," "It is my most mature work. My sole aim is to affirm that there is a brotherhood of man and that the individual has his place within that group."

Performing this masterpiece moved me so deeply that it would become a metaphor for my life. Years later I would go through the rigorous certification process at the Dance Notation Bureau in order to teach her dances, many of which have been preserved in dance notation. *Passacaglia* also inspired me to create Windhover, a place that supported communities of artists who lived and danced together in harmony—the underlying theme of this dance.

But this was to come later. First I knew I must dance in New York! So, with the blessing of my husband, whose enthusiasm for my dance career never wavered, I left for New York. (Herb followed several months later, having secured a position in a New York ad agency.)

(opposite) Doris Humphrey

CHAPTER 4

Good-bye Academia, Hello New York (1951)

Begin it now.

I took the train to the Big Apple not knowing where I would stay (with several friends in a loft), or how I would earn a living (proofreading), only that I would dance my heart out. And I did. I was lucky; in only a few weeks I was hired by choreographer Charles Weidman to dance in the City Center Opera Company. I did not mind being second fiddle to the singers who would invariably cross into our space or cover up our movements. I was getting paid to dance and that was enough!

Humphrey/Weidman Dance Group Poster

The years in New York City were as heady as drinking champagne. I was fortunate to be able to work with some of the greatest artists in dance: Jerome Robbins (*King and I*), José Limón, Charles Weidman, Jane Dudley, Helen Tamiris (*Plain and Fancy*), and Michael Kidd (*Can-Can*), to name a few.

But the two women who had the most powerful influence on me during my first years in the city were Doris Humphrey and Martha Graham, both giants in the world of modern dance. While I continued to take technique classes with José Limón, Doris offered me a scholarship to study composition with her. What she taught in that class became the content for her book on choreography, *The Art of Making Dances,* written shortly before her death and, in my view, one of the best books on dance composition ever written. I had learned and performed some of Doris' repertory the summer before, at Connecticut College, but that was just one aspect of her genius. Doris' composition class was a revelation. Her concepts were so simple, yet so powerful: space design; body design; time, metered or un-metered; dynamics. What could be more basic? Yet how many choreographers are totally unaware of these principles, so fundamental to movement!

Dancing in Doris' great works was a privilege and has continued to inspire me during the four decades of my own teaching and choreography. Doris Humphrey never raised her voice, never said more than was necessary, but what she did say was to the point. This was also true of her choreography, in keeping with her assertions that "The eye tires more quickly than the ear,"

Doris Humphrey in "New Dance"

Martha Graham in "Lamentation."

and that "most dances are too long." She encouraged us to look to other arts for inspiration, and she was a pioneer in the use of words and text with movement. These ideas continued to shape my own choreography, which has made use of the strong connections between the arts.

In addition, Doris introduced me to the Spanish poet and playwright Garcia Lorca through her masterful dances that used his poetry: "The Lament for Ignacio Sanchez Mejias" and "Dawn in New York." My love of Lorca's work eventually took me to Spain to study Flamenco and to create several works based on his poetry and plays.

Martha Graham's literally stunning presence as Jocasta, or Hecuba, was part of the siren call that wooed me away from academia and a secure job to the challenges of New York City. I studied with Martha in New York. Her studio was in an ordinary, barely-noticeable office building downtown on the West Side. Her school in the more upscale East 60s was still years away. I immediately enrolled in daily classes, then applied for a part-time job in a publishing house next door, the nearest I've ever been to making use of my college major, English literature and composition.

> *She sat in her chair like a priestess, like the Delphic oracle, penetrating you with those dark, deeply- set eyes that demanded your utmost allegiance. She spoke in tones and inflections that befitted an oracle, as if she received her messages from some unseen power. Her words and images seared our brains. "Why do you tilt your head?" Answer: " To expose the jugular vein as animals do when they wish to appear submissive." Or, "The spiral is a coil; the release is a retreat... hiss while you move through it, snarl as you retreat." Over and over she would remind us, "Movement never lies," and we believed her and felt we would rather die than be caught lying... When she was quiet it was worse. She could stare not at, but through you, and many times I left the class in tears even though she had not directed her criticism at me. It was the atmosphere—tense, concentrated, as though the fate of the world hung on our every gesture and, in Martha's eyes, it did.*

When she asked me into her company a few years later, I said no, but not because she ruled like a tyrant, but because by then I was happily dancing elsewhere. The commitment would have meant a year-long tour in Asia, and I could not see leaving my husband or my New York career for that length of time. However, I have regretted my decision—the only time I have said "no" to what would have been a once-in-a-lifetime experience with a choreographer and company that, at the time, was the greatest modern dance company in the world. I now tell my students, " I only regret what I didn't do, not what I did."

In my last appearance as a concert dancer, I performed Doris Humphrey's "New Dance" with the members of the Limón Company at The Brooklyn Academy of Music. It was a fitting end to my concert dance days in New York. After that, I auditioned for Jerome Robbins, who asked me to join the cast of a show called *King and I.* The prospect of earning a living through dance had great appeal...I became a Broadway hoofer.

CHAPTER 5

Broadway Hoofer (1952–1958)

My Broadway career began with a show called *The King and I* in 1952 and ended several years later at the North Shore Music theater in a show called *Carousel* where, pregnant with my first child, I danced the part of the ingenue lead, Louise. In between were many memorable moments, but none so etched in memory as the night I went on for Gwen Verdon in *Can-Can.*

We had just had a matinee performance and I had gone out to dinner and drinks with a friend. The show had opened the week before with rave reviews for the dancing overall and especially for the lead dancer, Gwen Verdon. She had become a star overnight. All of us in the chorus were so proud of her and the reviews confirmed what we knew: It was a dancer's show. With four difficult dance numbers plus lots of singing and staging, we were kept busy every minute and we loved it! In addition to my chorus part I was Gwen's understudy, but there'd been no time yet to rehearse her role—we'd been on the road in Boston and Philadelphia for six weeks and the show had been constantly re-written.

I drifted back to the Shubert Theater just in time, so I thought, to get ready for the evening performance.

In front of the theater is a crowd of people. "What's going on? Was there an accident?" I wonder. Then I recognize the director, the two producers, and the conductor—all facing in my direction. I look behind me. Nothing there. I look again and see the entire cast of the show. They are all staring at me. My walk slows, my heart begins to race. I must be hallucinating. What's happening? "Gwen's hurt her shoulder," I hear. "She's not performing tonight… You're on." Oh, no. I want to run in the other direction. Please don't let this be happening. This can't be true. "But she was fine in the matinee," I protest. "No, she hurt her shoulder in the Apache, took a bad fall, but covered it up. A real trooper. She finished the show in agony." "Some understudy I am," I think, "I didn't even notice."

Suddenly I am grabbed and taken bodily into the theater and placed on stage to face the entire

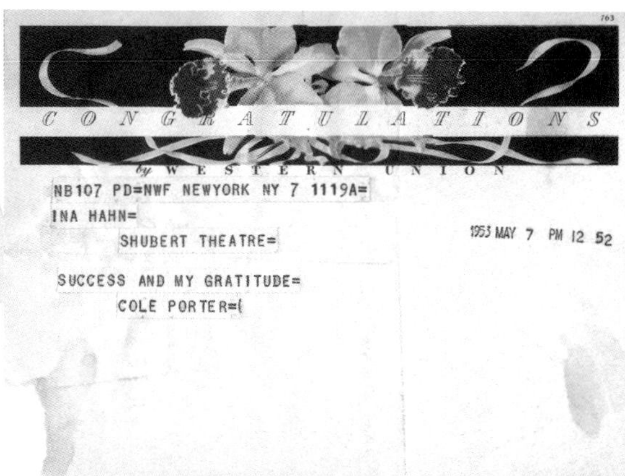

Telegram from Cole Porter

CAY-CAY

Can-Can Girl Back in Line After 2 Weeks Atop World

By MURIEL FISCHER,
Staff Writer.

Ina Hahn is back home today. Back in the basement dressing room of the Schubert Theater—where all the little chorus girls of "Can-Can" stay.

That dressing room's been home to Ina ever since the show opened here May 8. But somehow it's different—descending those stairs now. Somehow, her dancing feet keep moving her toward the star dressing room, the one right next to the stage. And she has to remind herself: It's all over now, you're back in the chorus again—but wasn't it nice. . . .

For two weeks, you see, young and pretty and talented Ina had lived an understudy's dream. What happened to Ina happens mostly in the movies—or is just dreamed of in basement dressing rooms.

'You're On, You're On!'

It was a night she'll never forget. "Wednesday, June 24. I was returning from dinner, and when I reached the stage door practically the whole cast was there waiting for me. All shrieking at once: 'You're on, you're on—you go on tonight!'"

Then came the details. Gwen Verdon, the show's featured dancer (and Broadway's newest dancing darling) had injured her shoulder during the matinee performance. Miss Hahn was her understudy.

Ina had only a half hour to dress (in *that* dressing room, the one right off the stage)—and half a million things to think about. A whole kaleidoscope of suddenly magical events of her 24-year lifetime passed before her eyes.

From Pigtails to B. A.

Like how she started balancing on her toes when she was a pigtailed 6-year-old in Boston. And how she pirouetted right through college. Wellesley, it was, and a B. A. degree in English lit—interrupted in her junior year while she danced down the marital aisle with Herbert Hahn, a Harvard man.

Then came the year of ballet teaching at Radcliffe College. And finally that trip to New York and the little apartment in Greenwich Village. While Mr. Hahn built up his advertising business, his brown-eyed, ebony-haired beauty studied ballet—and the chorus calls.

In retrospect, that first call, to the chorus of "The King and I" (June, 1952) was a prediction of things to come. Right away, In[a] was made an understudy—t[o] Simon of Legree in "The Sma[ll]

The Ina Hahn of yesterday—a star—is reflected in the mirror as the Ina Hahn of today—a member of the chorus line—prepares for her appearance in "Can-Can." United Press Photo.

House of Uncle Thomas" ballet. "But," she says pointingly, "I never went on."

Applause, Applause.

Quickly, while the curtain call stunned her into dazed readiness, she recalled the more recent events of her career: How she auditioned for Michael Kidd, the show's choreographer, last March, and how he chose her as Miss Verdon's understudy during the Philadelphia tryout. And how she never believed it really happened, that stars sometimes do get sick.

Then she was on the stage, kicking her legs high in the air, bumping and grinding through the "Garden of Eden" ballet. And ("alone, that is")—was bowing to that applause.

Some Day Again, Maybe.

It was all rather heady, she admits. "And terribly exciting."

And now it's all over. Miss Verdon has recovered and took over her original spot at yesterday's matinee. And Miss Hahn returned to the chorus.

"Oh, well," she sighs philosophically. "That the life of an understudy. You're on top one minute—unnoticed the next."

And off she went to the basement dressing room—to recount to eight other "Can-Can" chorus kickers how it felt to be a star. And once again dream with them

INA HAHN (Claudine) danced on Broadway in "The King and I," and understudied the Simon Legree role in the production's ballet, "Small House of Uncle Thomas." Her other Broadway credits include "Can-Can," in which she understudied Gwen Verdon, and "Plain and Fancy." She has appeared in "Carousel" at the North Shore Music Circus, and played her present role recently at the Paper Mill Playhouse. Miss Hahn has also danced in many television spectaculars.

orchestra, while the conductor bids me sing "If you love me truly," Gwen's vocal solo—the only one, thank God. "If only I can practice those lifts," I think, but the conductor insists I repeat the whole song with the orchestra in a new key. By then it's too late to do anything but put on make up and get into costume. "You're on," says the stage manager, pressing my shoulder. "Break a leg."

What can I say, except that I made it through the performance, thanks to the unbelievable professionalism and support of the entire company. Even the dreaded unrehearsed lifts were negotiated so I missed only one, and that was barely noticed, it went so fast. By the time Gwen returned to the show eight performances later, I had gotten so entrenched in the part I didn't want to give it up and go back to my fun, but humble chorus role. Needless to say, after that, even while performing my own part, my eyes were never off Gwen for a moment, and this proved wise because I went on many times after that—both in her role and as a lead dancer in other shows, far better prepared than I was that night.

Can-Can

Music and Lyrics: Cole Porter
Book and Direction: Abe Burrows
Choreography: Michael Kidd
Starring: Lilo and Peter Cookson
With: Hans Conried, Gwen Verdon, and Eric Rhodes

Clockwise from top left:
Ina with Eric Rhodes in the song "Come Along With Me"
High kicking finale of Can-Can
Ina as Claudine in the opening dance of Can-Can
(Ina with Gwen Verdon) in "The Garden of Eden Ballet"

CHAPTER 6

From Broadway, New York to Broadway, Rockport, Massachusetts (1958)

Maybe it was the call of the ocean that led us to Rockport, Massachusetts—my husband had a passion for sailing—or perhaps it was the promise we made ourselves many years before, in 1950, when we sailed into Rockport Harbor and fell in love with the town. That summer we rented a cottage on Bearskin Neck where I taught dance classes and Herb learned to lobster with the then harbormaster, Shorty Lesch. Our promise had been that we would someday return to Cape Ann to raise our children.

A decade had passed, but the desire was still strong. My first daughter, Lisa, was already a year old when Herb was offered a job in Boston that he couldn't refuse. So, as hard as it was for me to leave my career, I gave notice to the producers (I was about to begin rehearsals as lead dancer in *Pajama Game* at Paper Mill Playhouse in New Jersey) and we left the city of dreams for a place that seemed as removed from New York as Katmandu.

The Anawan, our Chesapeake Bay bug-eye ketch
(opposite) Ina Hahn auditioning for Plain and Fancy *before directors and choreographer Helen Tamiris.*

At first I felt isolated and stranded. But, within a few months, I was fortunate enough to meet a handful of women who had managed to combine lives of motherhood and art in such a creative and joyous way that I was inspired to do the same.

Virginia Burton Demetrios was founder and head of the Folly Cove Designers, whose original hand-block prints were famous nation-wide. Ginny, as she was called, was also a well-known children's book writer and illustrator, and even today her books are sought after and treasured. In fact, Boston Mayor Thomas Menino recently declared Saturday, November 13, 1999, "Mike Mulligan Day" in honor of the 60th anniversary of her popular story *Mike Mulligan and His Steam Shovel.*

Equally important to me, she loved dance. So, when she suggested I teach an adult class in my new studio, I was elated. My husband had in no time renovated what had been an old storage space on the third floor of One Center Street in Gloucester into a studio that was spacious and light-filled, with huge windows looking out onto Main Street and Gloucester Harbor. The class met every Wednesday morning and consisted primarily of painters and Folly Cove Designers, each with dedication and, thankfully, a great sense of humor regarding themselves as dancers. We laughed a lot.

I continued to teach at my Gloucester studio until 1968, when Windhover opened and it became impossible to keep up both places. But many of my students were able to take classes at Windhover, and several became day campers that first pioneering summer. As for my women's class, they would be lifelong friends who continued to inspire me as artists, and I would collaborate with one of them, Erma Wheeler, on many projects during the next ten years.

CHAPTER 7

Ina Hahn Dance Company (1960–1975)

Just below my studio on Center Street was the studio of artist Erma Wheeler and, after every class, I would go down to chat, look at her work, and watch her work. Through her art, so filled with the colors, images, and light of Cape Ann, I learned to see my new home in a fresh, exciting way.

What she and other Cape Ann artists were doing with color and design and paint, I wanted to do with my art. I re-read Doris Humphrey's book, *The Art of Making Dances*. Suddenly, all that she had taught me in those first years in New York came into focus. I began to experiment with movement. I formed a company of dancers and we collaborated with composers from the New England Conservatory to present original works throughout Cambridge and Boston. I began to choreograph for my own students at Windhover and for students at various colleges on the North Shore. In New York I danced other artists' choreography. Now I was able to find my own voice. It was an exhilarating new world.

A few years later, when I joined the faculty of The Boston Conservatory Dance Department, it was natural for me to turn to Erma Wheeler for advice on costumes, lighting, colors, and design. Her "Designs for Dance" are now part of the permanent collection at the Cape Ann Historical Museum in Gloucester which has a superb collection of works by renowned artists and sculptors who have worked on Cape Ann, and is an invaluable resource for Cape Ann's artistic heritage. So began a rich creative process for both of us during the sixties and seventies when Erma designed masks, slides, lighting and costumes for a host of works performed at the Loeb Theater and Sanders Theater at Harvard, Little Kresge at MIT, The Boston Conservatory, and other colleges in New England, as well as festivals in Portugal and Switzerland.

Erma Wheeler's watercolor costume design

Ina Hahn Company members rehearsing at Center Street, Gloucester, studio

Wheel of Fire

Music Collage: Marilyn Crispell
Choreography: Ina Hahn
Premiered at Boston Conservatory in 1972
Costumes and color design by Erma Wheeler

"I am bound upon a wheel of fire."
—Shakespeare, King Lear

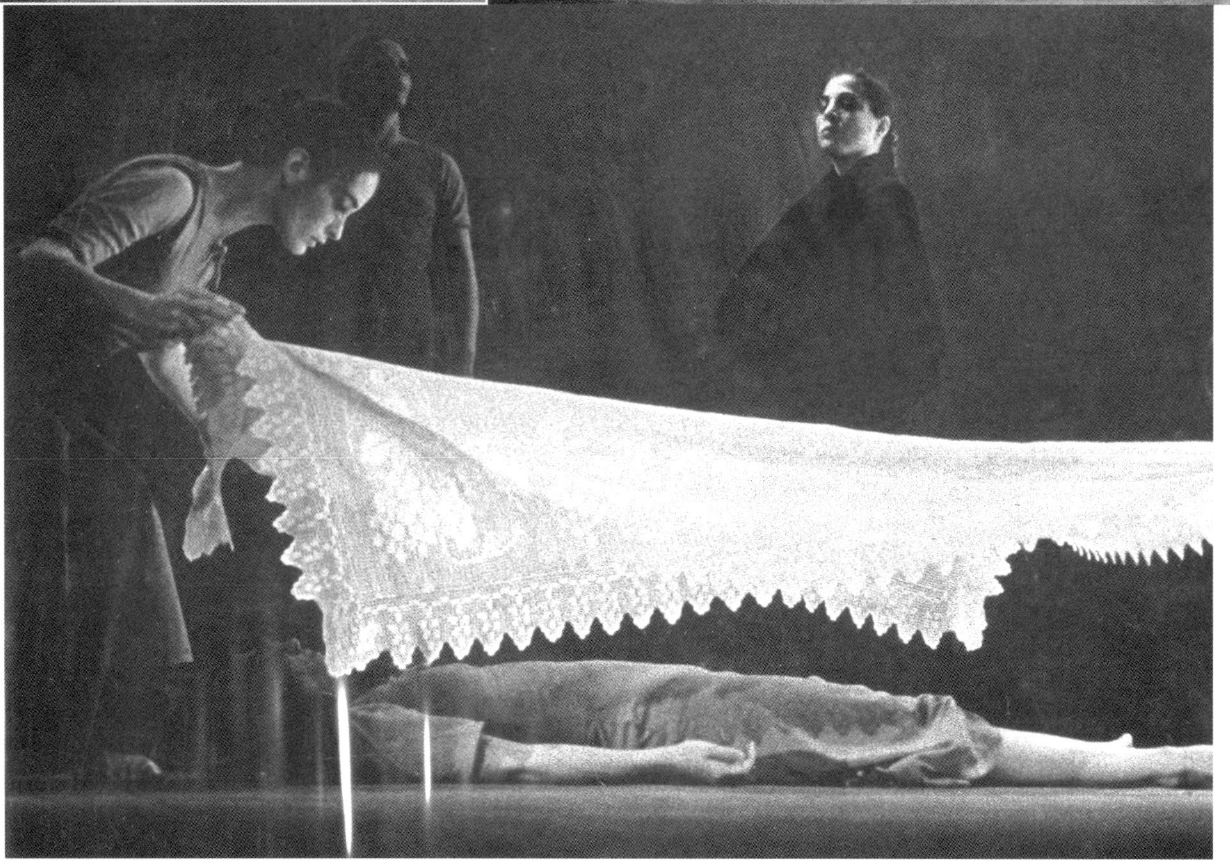

Boston Conservatory Dancers in "Wheel of Fire"

"Wheel of Fire" was inspired by Garcia Lorca's play, "The House of Bernada Alba." It is a drama about a matriarch who dominates her daughters in a household of formality and repression. The youngest daughter's love for Pepe El Romano, already betrothed to the eldest daughter, creates conflicts that terminate in tragedy.

Ever since "The House of Bernada Alba" was performed by the students at Windhover some time in the early seventies, I was haunted by it. Perhaps because I had three daughters, perhaps because I had recently been to Spain to visit Granada (where Lorca lived and wrote) and study Flamenco in Seville with a master, El Cojo.

The story stayed with me for a few years. Then I read an account of Lorca's death, how Franco's soldiers took him from his home into a woods and, without a word, shot him. He was still a young man and one of the greatest poets Spain has ever produced.

That was all I needed. I began working on "Wheel of Fire," and many years later wrote this poem to an artist who had so inspired me.

Mimi Kagin reviewed "Wheel of Fire" in *The Boston Globe* and said, "'Wheel of Fire', the new work by Ina Hahn, was performed with all the authority, strength, intensity and control the choreography required. These qualities are rare in professional dancers and are truly surprising in these young people. The work itself is a serious and often very moving dance drama with an interesting score by Marilyn Crispell."

"Wheel of Fire" was subsequently performed at the Lisbon Opera House in 1973 as well as in other theaters throughout the Northeast.

LORCA

Lorca…
Fredrico Garcia…
How I love your name.
Sounds—no—sings like
GRANADA, gypsy caves, guitars,
El Cojo teaching me the Sevillanas
In that long-ago cold studio
Where Pepe, in his grey overcoat and felt hat,
Rolled a cigarette on the yellow teeth of the piano,
Then played like a carved angel.

Your name spills with the blood
That came from her ebony throat—
That nameless canto singer of the deep song
Who haunts me still.
My feet hear her, stamping out the rhythms
Of Spain…
While my cupped and awkward hands
Struggle to clap in a foreign tongue.

You, Lorca, with your bells and fountains,
Your moon of mothers' milk and death,
Your voices of children like crickets in the night,
You, who cared for the simplest things…
They caught you, like any nymph
In their web,
And they crushed you.

Was it precisely at five in the afternoon?
…At five o'clock in the afternoon…
If so, who wailed for you?
…At five o'clock in the afternoon…
Did the clock stop or miss one beat?
Hold its breath for a second?
…At five o'clock…
Did the earth shudder
As their rifles poured forth venom upon you?
…in the afternoon…Did the mountains spew fire?

What happened?
Of all you praised with such skill and beauty
Did not one step forth and cry out?
No river, tree, rider…
No wind to mark the moment,
Or silence to honor it?
Not even a pause in the music?
No.
Castanets kept clicking,
Fountains leapt and played,
Though your blood cried out
When they took you to the countryside and shot you
Even the stars didn't blink an eye.

Nothing happened…
And everything.

The Unicorn, The Gorgon, and The Manticore

By Gian Carlo Menotti
Performed in 1972 at Sanders Theater, Harvard
with The Cecilia Society
Conductor: Donald Teeters
Choreography: Ina Hahn
Cast: The Man in the Castle, Tom Molinaro
The Count, Mark Thompson
The Countess, Beth Soll
The Unicorn, Patricia Walker
The Gorgon, Guy Peartree
The Manticore, Louis Moreno
Townspeople: Dance students from the Boston Conservatory
Mask design and execution: Erma Wheeler

Clockwise from top left:
The Man and the Unicorn
The Count and Countess
The Man and the Manticore

Ellen Pfeifer wrote in *The Boston Globe*, "The evening was delightful—a charming expedition into a world where shy unicorns are numerous and desired as status symbols...The witty, forceful dance-mime created by Ina Hahn subtly reflected the text and responded well to the music."

Louis Snyder wrote, "Menotti has provided an ingratiating score which had been prepared musically by director Donald Teeters, with inventive choreography by Ina Hahn...aided by excellent performances from the three title characters as well as the man and the count and countess."

The Gorgon

Section Two

THE PLACE

C H A P T E R 8

The Farm in Pigeon Cove (1967)

"But I don't know how to farm," I protested... "Don't worry," he assured me, "I'll build you a dance center."

In 1967, Herbert and I purchased the last farm in Pigeon Cove, a small village by the sea some two miles north of the town of Rockport. The five acre farm included a main house, a cow barn and hayloft, stables, a slaughter house, various out-buildings, and pasture land.

In less than a year, during a winter that broke records for snow, Herb Hahn converted barn into dance studio, stable into library and music room, sheds and outbuildings into dormitories, and renovated the main house so it could serve as a dining and kitchen complex. The task would have been difficult enough for a full-time crew of builders and carpenters. Herb had neither at his disposal.

A teacher and head of the English department at Manchester High School, Herb had little free time, nor was he experienced in the construction of buildings. What he had was super-human energy and a dream. Working after school and long into the night, raiding the length and breadth of Massachusetts' North Shore for architectural treasures, he created a mini-New England village replete with hand-hewn beams, barn siding, statuary, stained glass windows, wrought iron gates and railings, railroad lanterns, cupolas, gothic spires, and ships' bells.

The bell tower on the music barn, formerly the stable

*Two of the cabins,
Woodnymph and Tiffany*

Herb Hahn building the cupola on the barn

Six months later, in June of 1968, the performing and creative arts camp for girls was ready to open. We decided to name the place after one of our favorite poems, "To A Windhover," written by Gerard Manley Hopkins. The "windhover" in Hopkins' poem is a kestrel, a small falcon much like our seagull, notable for hovering in the air with its head against the wind. Its flight is described in the poem as symbolic of the soaring of man's imagination and the spiritual quest that informs great art.

The winter of 1967–68; a view of the farm

The music barn

Suburbia

The Hahn family in 1971: Ina, Herb, Lisa, Pamela, Lauri, and the ever-present collies

"I remember the manure... it was piled sky-high outside the stables, as big as a mountain—or so it seemed to my sister and me. We had to shovel it with pitchforks every afternoon after school, and we piled it into dumpsters that Dad would cart off. We earned money for this and were promised horses as rewards. We were told it was good training for having our own horses, but I was skeptical about the new farm Mom and Dad had bought...So much manure!"

— Lisa Hahn, 11 years

The theater with its wide barn boards

C H A P T E R 9

Windhover . . .
for the performing and creative arts (1968–1984)

WINDHOVER CREDO: Young people are instinctively creative. Every child begins as a maker of games doing what comes naturally in a free and spontaneous expression of the play instinct. The making of dances, plays, paintings, sculpture, and music is a continuation of that same instinct. But as the child matures, that instinct must be reinforced by training and discipline in the service of a craft. To work daily with the materials of one's art, to experience the sweat and frustration as well as the joy in giving form to one's ideas is to begin to understand a good deal about art, about life, about oneself... To pursue perfection is to pursue an unattainable ideal. But in the pursuit of the ideal begins responsibility, and in responsibility begins freedom. That special freedom, won through discipline and devotion, is what we seek to achieve at Windhover.

Because my husband and I believed strongly in an education in the arts and because such a comprehensive art education for young people (we had three daughters by then) was unavailable elsewhere on the North Shore, we decided that Windhover would focus equally on all the arts, not just dance. The courses at Windhover included: dance: modern, jazz, ballet, and choreography; theater: acting and set design; painting; ceramics; music: instrumental and choral; writing; and literature.

In the summer of 1968, Windhover opened as an arts camp for teenage girls. The first season had a wondrous sense of adventure. The thirty students who attended that eight-week session had the energy and commitment of true pioneers. They were a mix of local dance students from my Center Street Studio in Gloucester, students of Herb's from Manchester High

Practicing ballet on wagon wheels

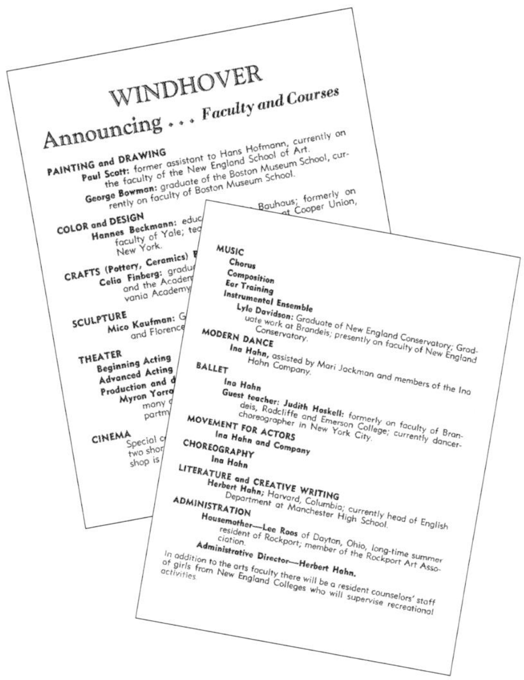

WINDHOVER

Announcing . . . *Faculty and Courses*

PAINTING and DRAWING
Paul Scott: former assistant to Hans Hofmann, currently on the faculty of the New England School of Art.
George Bowman: graduate of the Boston Museum School, currently on faculty of Boston Museum School.

COLOR and DESIGN
Hannes Beckmann: educ... Bauhaus; formerly on faculty of Yale; tea... at Cooper Union, New York.

CRAFTS (Pottery, Ceramics)
Celia Finberg: gradu... and the Academ... vania Academy...

SCULPTURE
Mico Kaufman: G... and Florence...

THEATER
Beginning Acting
Advanced Acting
Production and d...
Myron Yorra... many ... partm...

CINEMA
Special c... two shor... shop is...

MUSIC
Chorus
Composition
Ear Training
Instrumental Ensemble
Lyle Davidson: Graduate of New England Conservatory; Graduate work at Brandeis; presently on faculty of New England Conservatory.

MODERN DANCE
Ina Hahn, assisted by Mari Jackman and members of the Ina Hahn Company.

BALLET
Ina Hahn
Guest teacher: Judith Haskell: formerly on faculty of Brandeis, Radcliffe and Emerson College; currently dancer-choreographer in New York City.

MOVEMENT FOR ACTORS
Ina Hahn and Company

CHOREOGRAPHY
Ina Hahn

LITERATURE and CREATIVE WRITING
Herbert Hahn; Harvard, Columbia; currently head of English Department at Manchester High School.

ADMINISTRATION
Housemother—Lee Roos of Dayton, Ohio, long-time summer resident of Rockport; member of the Rockport Art Association.
Administrative Director—Herbert Hahn.

In addition to the arts faculty there will be a resident counselors' staff of girls from New England Colleges who will supervise recreational activities.

The first season's schedule of classes
(opposite) The sheer joy of movement

Outdoor stage in the garden

School, several from around the North Shore (I had taught at Bradford and Endicott Colleges), and from Boston, where my company frequently performed. I had no trouble finding outstanding faculty and counselors, drawn from musicians at the New England Conservatory with whom I had collaborated, dancers from my company, artists, and even a theater director from Cape Ann. And, of course, Herb Hahn directed the writing and literature courses.

From the start there was always a special sense of community which extended beyond the courses and intensive training, beyond the friendships and bonds formed—several ending in marriage. Many campers returned year after year, often coming back as counselors when they became old enough.

During its seventeen summers, Windhover was filled to capacity. Students came from the USA, Canada, Europe, and Mexico to attend its unique programs. Over the years, new buildings were added, including a theater/chapel, where Herb used colonial paneling, barn boards, and stained glass windows from a private memorial chapel in Prides Crossing. A second dance studio was built to accommodate the increased enrollment, and, finally, an outdoor stage for dance and theater performances.

Lisa Hahn as Cassandra in Trojan Women

The following excerpts from an article written by Harriet Webster in *The New England Coastal Journal* in 1983 describe vividly her impressions of a visit to Windhover:

"Stepping through the purple loosestrife, the Queen Anne's lace, and the goldenrod, you seem to feel the music before you hear it. As you come closer to the cluster of wood and stone buildings, you realize that the sounds have more than one source. The Schumann comes from the second story dance studio, the ragtime from the music building, and somewhere out of sight a couple of young voices sing out the theme song from "Fame."

The girls who hurry past walk taller than most teenagers. They talk with their hands and most of them wear their hair pulled back from their faces, making their features unusually expressive. Many wear leotards and leg warmers. These are summer campers, but instead of honing their skills in softball, archery, and tennis, they study dance, theater, music and art.

But that was just the beginning. Windhover looks like the kind of place lovely things almost have to happen. The special touches—chandeliers in the studios, a birdbath just waiting for a robin, a handsome cupola that crowns a barn—hint at the temperament of the people who come here to work and play.

As you wander the grounds, stepping into some of the dozen buildings, the picture comes into focus. In the theater, an instructor discusses the differences between emphatic, artistic, and unconscious gestures. A small knot of girls stationed by the door giggles over a potential trouble spot in the Renaissance comedy "The Knight of the Burning Pestle" they are preparing for production.

Just as you begin to think that these kids are a shade too serious, a shade too mature, a mite too intense, you see the outdoor blackboard where the day's menu is posted. "Dinner—chili," it reads, but just below someone has added "fried frog hearts." You laugh and begin to realize that these kids are working hard not because they're drudges but because they're enjoying it, because they're having fun. And that's exactly the way Ina Hahn wants it to be. The girls go swimming and horseback riding and she admits that by the end of the session many of the campers could provide an accurate inventory of just about every shop on Bearskin Neck."

Character, Jenny, belts out a song in Kurt Weill's Three Penny Opera

Ready for miles of trails in Dogtown

(above) *New England Conservatory composer, Lyle Davidson, coaches flutists (Lauri Hahn in front)*

(right) *Just graduated from Williams College, young Joe Mulholland directs and accompanies the campers.*

Cooling off on The Anawan

"When I was 8 years old, my parents bought Windhover. I was so disappointed. I had been looking forward to going away to summer camp for years—like my sisters. Disappointment soon faded away, however, in all the excitement of that first summer and the many that followed. I remember agonizing each summer over my class schedule. It was impossible to fit in modern and ballet dance classes every morning if I also wanted to take theater and painting, the latter being a 3 hour class where we would go all over Cape Ann to paint various beautiful landscapes. The afternoons were crammed as full as possible with flute lessons, music theory, printmaking, pottery, batik, or mime. I so wanted to do it all! Then of course later in the afternoon we would swim at the beach, horseback ride, or sign up for the ever-popular sailing on the Anawan, a 45 foot Chesapeake Bay ketch. And then there was a choice between a trip to Bearskin Neck to shop or the movies at night, if you didn't have play rehearsal.

What also made the summers so special was the wonderful assortment of people who came to teach and learn. The other campers were such a savvy and diverse group. Many were from the New York City area and seemed so knowledgeable to me in the ways of the world. I remember being riveted by their stories, true and made-up, and raucous jokes late at night after lights out. Over twenty years later I still maintain some close friendships with girls I met during camp. Looking back, I realize how incredible our faculty was. We had truly great and renowned artists, dancers, theater professors, and musicians as our mentors. I loved to play the flute and every summer I would make such great strides in my ability that my teacher during the school year would be amazed. My excitement for music increased enormously every summer. It's really no wonder that the thought of going away to camp never crossed my mind again after that first summer at Windhover. I enjoyed being a camper for 9 years, then later came back to teach theater and direct plays for 2 wonderful fun-filled summers."

—Lauri Hahn

Steady hands and concentration

Future artist

• Love and art at Windhover center

Continued from page 3

and two children spent her vacation at Windhover and became so excited about pursuing dance professionally that at the end of the program she asked her husband, "What do you think of me not going back to my job?"

"We're trying to attract a serious group of people," Mulholland says.

"Ina asks students, 'Why are you dancing? Because you love it or because you want to be famous?' ."

"It's a healthy atmosphere," Wise adds. "It affects your lifestyle."

Mulholland and Wise live in Boston during the year and can't understand why anyone would want to stay in the city during the summer when there is the option of coming to a place like Windhover, situated near Rockport quarries and the ocean and occupying the site of a former farm.

The farm's original slaughterhouse, along with a number of other small wood-shingled buildings house the ballet and modern dance studios and the theater hall. They form an intimate circle — surrounded by shade trees — which include the outdoor stage with its Greek motifs of statues and white columns.

A unique aspect of the performance series is its association with a master class series. Most of the artists who come to Windhover to perform also lead classes in their craft. The New York Lyric Circus, for example, which performed last weekend, gave a workshop on circus arts.

The performing arts center still has much planned for the rest of the summer. At 8 p.m. Saturday, Julie Ince Thompson, a solo artist, will present a theater-dance production based on a book about Tamsen Donner, a pioneer woman who survived a tragic expedition out west.

On Aug. 14 and 15, students will present an original adaption of Percy MacKaye's verse-play "Dogtown Common," basing its characters on the inhabitants and lives of the settlers wh lived in the heart of Cape Ann.

The last of three two-weel classses begins July 27 and wil focus on "A Mixed Approach t Dance-Drama."

Despite Windhover's schedule, Mulholland and Wise sa they will continue to stay a Windhover — where they live i a converted horse stable — "until it's too cold."

"I have been returning to Windhover for over thirty years and have developed a warm, personal feeling of "coming home," and also a feeling of the most creative haven that any artist can experience. As a young student, I was constantly inspired by all my teachers and the performers who danced on the outdoor stage with nature's woods as a backdrop... To see myself returning as a teacher and challenging myself to give back the same love and quality to all the new students continues the Windhover tradition. I will always remember how Windhover has given me the opportunity and high standards which are required in such a competitive art... the one adjective consistently used by everyone to describe this wonderful place is 'Magical'."

—Pamela Wise

Pamela Wise was 11 years old when she started Windhover as a camper in 1968. She has never lost her connection to it, either as a student, a teacher, or a performer. She even met her husband, composer-musician Joe Mulholland, when they were teaching at Windhover and they celebrated their marriage here. She directed the dances for our July, 2000 Windhover Dance Retrospective, "Moving Forward, Looking Back."

File photo

Pamela Wise, Joseph Mulholland and a friend on the grounds of Windhover.

(opposite) Eleven-year-old Pamela Wise, leaping off the dunes at Wingaersheek Beach

CHAPTER 10

And Death Shall Have No Dominion (1975)

"And death shall have no dominion…"
—Dylan Thomas

Herbert Hahn, co-founder and builder of Windhover, died in April 1975. He was 51 years old and his last days were spent building the arbor in the garden, which has since seen hundreds of dance, theater, and music performances, as well as weddings. It seems totally fitting that this man of such energy and originality built his own memorial. Not that he meant it to be one. What he had in mind was exactly what it has become…a place of magic in which to create magic.

By 1975, the camp did have a life of its own, and it went on that summer and for ten more, just as he would have wished. The Windhover poem is dedicated "To Christ, Our Lord." It is about flight, about a bird that hovers in the air, soars, and then falls. But when it falls it does not die, it "gashes gold-vermilion," a reference to the Resurrection. I believe it was no accident that Windhover's name was chosen from this poem because Windhover, too, was resurrected. This theme of re-birth and re-generation continued throughout the years and into the present, as Windhover spread its wings to seek out new challenges and goals, and to attract the people who would realize them.

The garden

(above) Richard Winik, center, with the ball
(right) Richard Winik, captain of the basketball team

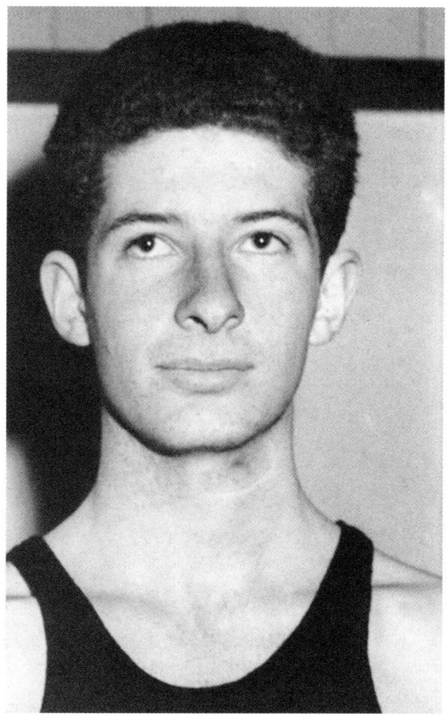

Perhaps the best example of Windhover's continual rebirth came in the person of Richard Winik. As if sent by the angels, he appeared in the summer of 1976, a man who would become indispensable to the continuation of Windhover. At first he seemed an unlikely person to be involved in an arts camp for girls. He was a film photographer who had spent his life as cameraman, editor, director, and producer of sports films.

I had met Richard Winik in the fifties when we lived in the same apartment house in Riverdale, New York. I was then dancing in *The King and I* at the St. James Theater and he was filming basketball games at Madison Square Garden—both night-time jobs, so we often drove into the city together. Our lives and commitments led us in different directions after that period, but we always kept in touch. It was one of those friendships meant to endure, and it has!

In 1970, Dick formed his own company—W&W Films—which acted as the film division of Major League Baseball. He produced the NBA and NHL championship films and made annual promotional films for the Mets, the Cosmos, the Army football team, the New York Racing Association, and the United States Tennis Association. He also produced the U.S. Open golf film and received a Peabody Award for his work on the "Baseball World of Joe Garagiola" pre-game show. Company personnel also received Emmys or Emmy nominations for editing or camerawork on several features shown on NBC.

Since 1976, this legendary sports film photographer has been the chief and only landscaper of five acres of grass, trees, fields, and gardens that comprise a place of uneven terrain with granite outcroppings everywhere. Commuting from NYC every two or three weeks, he manages to mow every scrap of lawn each spring and summer, rake every leaf each fall and early spring, and cut down or prune trees when necessary. Only once, when he was ill, did I hire anyone to fill in for him. Two young men didn't do half the job that Dick, a perfectionist, accomplishes alone. Since then, I have never had to hire a gardener or landscaping company; in fact, when I've tried, Dick insists I don't need to. He's right. But I still can't believe how he does it—nor can anyone else.

Dick has also videoed every performance at Windhover, with an eye for movement that is unsurpassed. As Martha Graham said when she chose him to film her work, "I want someone who knows where the action is," and he does, even before it happens. Add to this his role as parking attendant for performances or weddings and you have a spirit and energy without which Windhover could not have existed for the past 25 years—given voluntarily, out of love.

Autumn: One of four statues in the garden, each representing a season

American Gothic: Landscaper par excellence

Concerto

Music: Bach, Brandenburg Concerto #6
Choreography: Ina Hahn
First commissioned by the Harvard Summer School and performed at Sanders Theater in 1976
Re-staged for dancers from The Boston Conservatory in 1977
Performances in 1995 by Windhover Dancers at Windhover and with The Cape Ann Symphony in Gloucester

The Sunday Herald American's review of the Conservatory performance in April 1977 ran, "Most pleasing of the works shown was Ina Hahn's lyrical, balletic 'Concerto'...Set to Bach's 'Brandenburg Concerto No. 6', Hahn's choreography is expansive, free-flowing and upbeat—the kind of movement young students perform simply, joyously, and well. With an open, easy gait, legs scissor across the stage, the dancers embracing space...In the second movement, the emphasis on gestures of supplication and celebration makes 'Concerto' a work with a spiritual mood. The strength of line in this piece, the temperate, gentle spirit of the three movements worked well for the students."

The connections between the arts has been all important for me, from the poetry of Lorca, which inspired "Wheel of Fire," to the "Pieta" of Michaelangelo, which became the dominant image of "Cycle."

My love for Bach extends back into my childhood when I was blessed with a piano teacher who taught me not just piano technique but also how to hear and differentiate the forms of Western music—whether canon or fugue, sonata form or theme and variation, ABA, and all the rest. When I was only eleven or twelve, he started me on the Bach Inventions and so began my love affair with Bach that is renewed every time I hear a Bach piece. I think Bach teaches one to hear—really hear. All those voices, all that sound going on at once, yet making sense—and never going on too long. What's more, he knew how to write (or re-write) a good melody. I still remember the Bach tunes I sang to myself as I walked the two miles to my lesson every Sunday.

When the Harvard Summer Dance program commissioned me to choreograph a piece for their professional dance company in 1976, I had just been through a year of mourning. I had focused on death and loss. Now I wanted to make a dance that would celebrate life, with all its energy, gaiety, and spirituality. Throughout the year I had been listening to the Brandenburg Concertos, written during some of the happiest years of Bach's life at the court of Prince Leopold, where he had the best musicians in Germany at his disposal. Would I dare to take one of these masterpieces by a composer I so revered and use it for my own vision? I had been given some of the best dancers in Boston and New York to work with. Why not try?

Whatever you can do, or dream you can do,
begin it.

In two weeks of intense rehearsals with these great dancers the Brandenburg Concerto #6 was finished.

(opposite) Boston Conservatory Dancers in "Concerto"

CHAPTER 11

Transition: The Pre-Professional Program in Dance (1980–1985)

In the early 1980s, Windhover extended its camp program for teenage girls to include a special pre-professional dance program which ran concurrently with the six-week camp session. This grew out of the need for a more intense curriculum for the advanced students who wished to pursue careers in dance. Many of them are now in professional companies in New York; some are dancing in Broadway shows while others teach and choreograph.

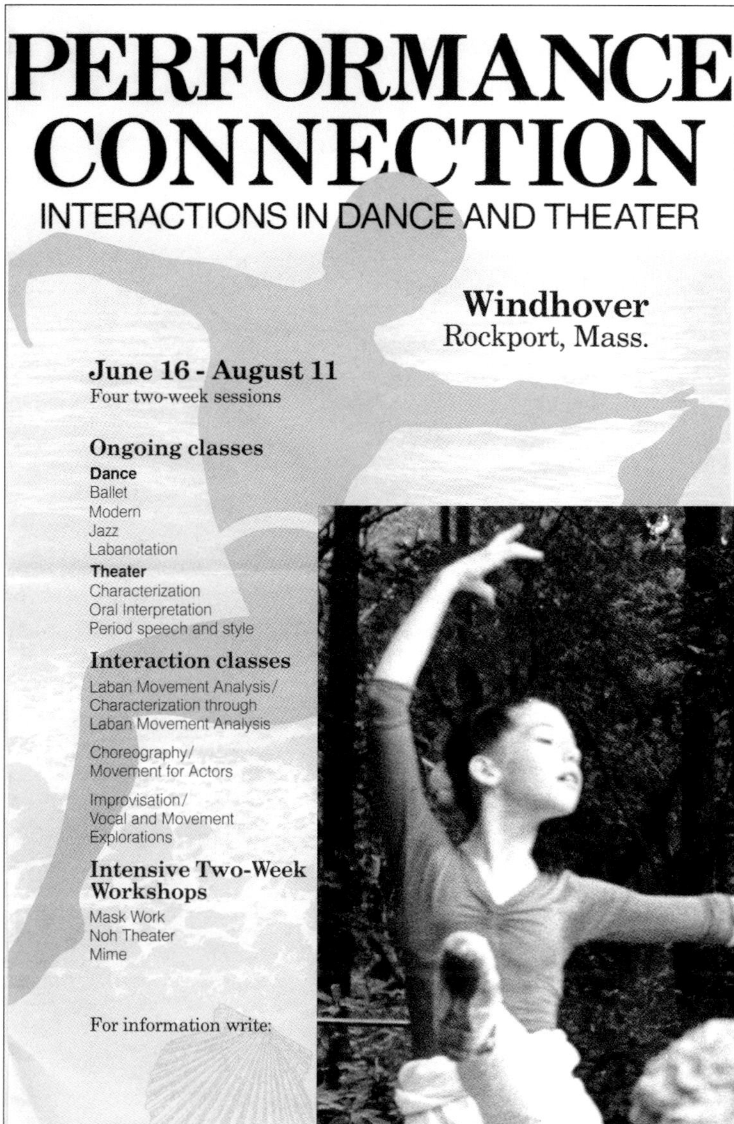

PERFORMANCE CONNECTION

INTERACTIONS IN DANCE AND THEATER

Windhover
Rockport, Mass.

June 16 - August 11
Four two-week sessions

Ongoing classes

Dance
Ballet
Modern
Jazz
Labanotation

Theater
Characterization
Oral Interpretation
Period speech and style

Interaction classes

Laban Movement Analysis/
Characterization through
Laban Movement Analysis

Choreography/
Movement for Actors

Improvisation/
Vocal and Movement
Explorations

Intensive Two-Week Workshops

Mask Work
Noh Theater
Mime

For information write:

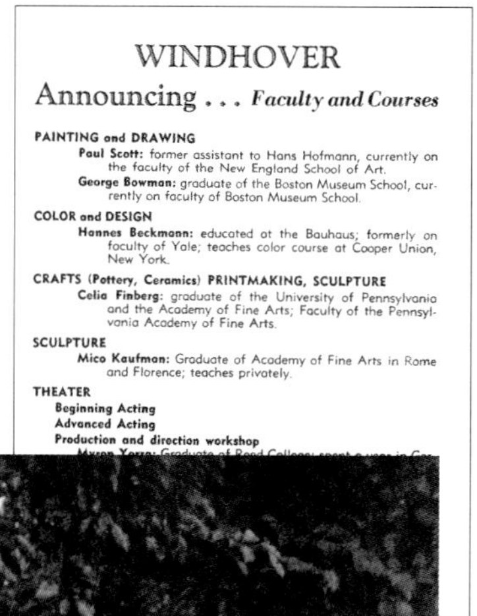

WINDHOVER

Announcing . . . *Faculty and Courses*

PAINTING and DRAWING

Paul Scott: former assistant to Hans Hofmann, currently on the faculty of the New England School of Art.

George Bowman: graduate of the Boston Museum School, currently on faculty of Boston Museum School.

COLOR and DESIGN

Hannes Beckmann: educated at the Bauhaus; formerly on faculty of Yale; teaches color course at Cooper Union, New York.

CRAFTS (Pottery, Ceramics) PRINTMAKING, SCULPTURE

Celia Finberg: graduate of the University of Pennsylvania and the Academy of Fine Arts; Faculty of the Pennsylvania Academy of Fine Arts.

SCULPTURE

Mico Kaufman: Graduate of Academy of Fine Arts in Rome and Florence; teaches privately.

THEATER

Beginning Acting
Advanced Acting
Production and direction workshop

Anina von Molnar

Anina von Molnar, pre-professional dancer who went on to become professional

May, 1985

The day replays
Again and again,
Yielding its sting—
And the same deep pain.

Beyond all words is the death of one's child . . . beyond all grief.

Pamela Hahn on her white horse, Pina
(opposite) Drawing by Pamela Hahn at age 14 years

Pamela Hahn was one of the most imaginative and talented young artists and writers I have ever known. At age nine she spent her summer writing and illustrating three books; at age 11 she gave me a collection of her poems for Christmas. The collection of nine poems is titled "My Secret Place" and on the following page is the title poem .

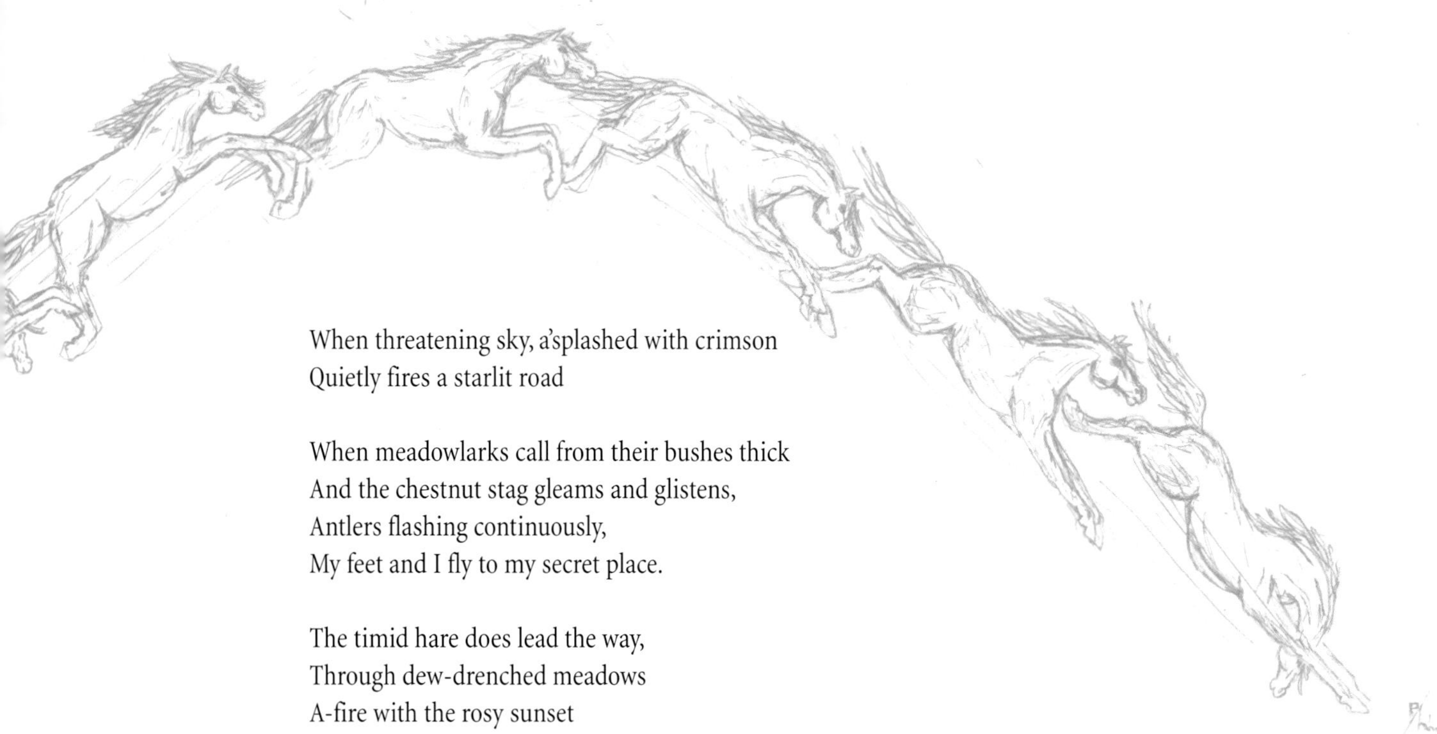

When threatening sky, a'splashed with crimson
Quietly fires a starlit road

When meadowlarks call from their bushes thick
And the chestnut stag gleams and glistens,
Antlers flashing continuously,
My feet and I fly to my secret place.

The timid hare does lead the way,
Through dew-drenched meadows
A-fire with the rosy sunset
And my secret place seems to welcome me—
Silent and friendly, wild and majestic
And all, yes all
My very own.

Oh, come with me to my Secret Place
Come. I'll lead the way.

—Pamela Hahn, 11 years

For Pam from Jeff Archenbault

She and her horse
change eyes
and mingle their strides
She straddles his flank
and tightens her thighs

Both bloods run together

The pounding of hooves
vibrate through the air
A sunset drowns
in the floods of her hair.

"Requiem," a dance created by Ina Hahn in memory of Pamela Hahn.

Pigeon Cove Harbor, photo by boatowner Peter Prybot

"Six Big Guys In A Little-Ass Boat"

Miss Marina and The Representative dancing a tango in "The American Way"

The Fish in "The Gear," a rap song (below) Pamela Wise and Sandee Havunen as fish in "The Gear" song

The Battle for Pigeon Cove Harbor, an original musical celebrating the victory of the Pigeon Cove boatowners over the developers who planned to take away their moorings and their access to the harbor. "This work resonates the theme of the times: the integrity of people's lifeblood, work, culture, history, threatened by big money."

—Patryc Wiggins

"Las Meninas Variations" (1988) was inspired by the paintings of Pablo Picasso. In 1957, Picasso did forty-four variations of "Las Meninas" (The Maids of Honor), painted by the 17th-century artist, Velasquez. Twenty-two of the variations were the basis for this dance, which features music by David Alpher.

(left) The painting "Las Meninas" (Ladies-in Waiting) by Velasquez
(below) Dancers against the slide of Velasquez'painting

(above) Eden Mazer, center, as The Princess (Enfanta)
(right) Picasso's first variation on "Las Meninas"

Erma's watercolor designs of costumes and masks for "The Unicorn, The Gorgon, and The Manticore"

Erma Wheeler's watercolor sketch of "Wheel of Fire"

Erma Wheeler's artistry and strong visual sense was an inspiration as we collaborated on these and many other dances. Her imaginative designs of masks, costumes, slides, and lighting for several of my dances are now part of the permanent collection at the Cape Ann Historical Society.

Sandee Havunen

Photo by John Blanding

Doris Humphrey's *Water Study* is performed in silence—the dancers' breathing and the wind through the trees behind the stage provide the only accompaniment.

"Water Study" performed on Windhover stage

Clockwise from top:
The outdoor stage flanked by statues
The garden with trellis
Ina's grandson, Herbert Lawrence, one year old

Ina's granddaughter, Pamela Lawrence, age 3

Windhover's Theater/Chapel (below) A stained-glass window in the theater

Photo by John Blanding

"Shakers" choreographed by Doris Humphrey in 1931.

"Shakers," choreographed in 1931 by Doris Humphrey, is based on the means by which the Shaker sect believed they could literally shake off their sins. In Shaker communities the men and women did not intermingle. So too, in the dance, there is an imaginary line down the center dividing the sexes.

Section Three

THE VISION

CHAPTER 12

Windhover Spreads Its Wings (1985–2000 and beyond)

"I was impressed not only by the quality and complexity of the work, but also by the extent to which your group has integrated history, dance/drama/ music, and philosophical/cultural issues within single pieces. What your group is doing at Windhover is clearly the fulfillment of a significant artistic and educational vision. I think it is unique and important work."

—Donald W. Oliver
Professor of Education
Harvard University Graduate School of Education

1984 was the final year of Windhover as a camp. Though the programs were successful and the camp had been filled to capacity for 17 years, I was too devastated by the loss of my daughter to continue running it in 1985, the year of her death.

Once again, people who cared about Windhover—artists, dancers, friends—rallied and together, we crafted a mission statement, formed a Board for the newly incorporated non-profit foundation, and created a new vision which would expand both our programs and our outreach.

Margaret Beals

Our mission, stated in the Windhover Bulletin of 1988: To provide the highest quality training through classes and workshops; to continue to sponsor outstanding artists in performance at affordable prices; to create original works which reflect and utilize the talents and rich artistic resources in the area and which focus on the interaction of dance, theater, music, and the visual arts.

We initiated workshops and classes for older students and adults as well as young aspiring artists; we created and performed works in dance and theater that used the local artistic talent of the community and found themes that reflected the interests and concerns of the community. Some of the dance/theater works we produced in the 1980s were: *Dogtown Common; Peer Gynt*; and "Hannah and The Hatchet Gang," based upon Kitty Parson's book about the women who, on July 8, 1857, ensured that Rockport would be a dry town forever. Years later, in the 1990s, that battle would be fought again, with "Hannah Lives" on many a bumper sticker in Town. Hannah won again: Rockport is still dry.

Windhover became both a resource and venue for performing artists in the area; we explored new forms and ways to combine the arts. For example, throughout "Las Meninas," choreographed and performed in 1988, slides of Velasquez and Picasso paintings were shown in concert with the movement, as a means of heightening the drama. (*See pages 70–71*)

"Negro Spirituals," choreographed by Helen Tamiris

We also formed a Windhover Dance Company which was invited to perform in Boston and at colleges in the Northeast. Windhover's Dance Connection Company of professional dancers from Massachusetts' North Shore performed several masterpieces by pioneer American choreographers, including Charles Weidman; Doris Humphrey; and Helen Tamiris, whose suite, "Negro Spirituals," from the 1940s, was one of the first dances that addressed the racial divide in America.

Believing strongly in bringing together local and community artists with professionals from New York and Boston, we invited guest artists who were outstanding in their fields to teach and to perform at Windhover each summer.

Clockwise from top left:
Elena Martinson and Andrei Ustinov
Jaclynn Villamil
Nicole and Jamie Huggins in "The Pursued"
Patricia Adams

Some of the performers included:

- Trent Arterberry in performances of mime
- Solo actress/dancer Julie Ince Thompson in her award-winning "Tamsen Donner"
- Margaret Beals in several evening-long solo performances
- Skip LaPlante, musician-composer, in an evening of "Music for Homemade Instruments"
- Deena Burton, performer of Indonesian dance/drama
- Jaclynn Villamil, New York performer and teacher
- Carl Thomsen, director of Dancer's Courageous in Gloucester
- Patricia Adams in "Dances of Isadora Duncan"
- Jose Mateo's Ballet Theater of Boston
- Boston-based performers Nicole and Jamie Huggins in Joseph Gifford's "The Pursued."

Outstanding Windhover faculty included:

- George Angell, director and theater department faculty at Hillsdale College, director of Windhover's theater program for five years, and responsible for the original staging of *Peer Gynt, Dogtown Common,* and other dance/ theater works
- Anamarie Sarazin, principal dancer of the Boston Ballet
- Jimmy Viera, jazz dancer and Boston choreographer
- Lance Westergard, ballet master for Joffrey II Dancers and the recipient of two choreographic fellowships from the National Endowment for the Arts.

Lance Westergard

Kay Cummings, chairperson of the dance and theater department at NYU who directed various Windhover theater workshops during the '80s wrote:

> *"Windhover provides a nurturing environment for artists and those who wish to explore their artistic gifts... in a place ideally suited to that purpose... It is both unique and inspiring."*

Windhover workshops and instructors have included:

- Lynn Simonson, master teacher of the Simonson jazz dance technique and founder/director of New York's Dancespace, has directed workshops at Windhover since 1992.
- Betty Jones taught a workshop in Humphrey-Limón Technique. Betty Jones was a principal soloist in José Limón's Company, best known for her performance of Desdemona in Limón's masterpiece, "The Moor's Pavanne."
- Risa Steinberg, former soloist with the Limón Company and called 'one of our great modern dancers', gave "A Celebration of Dance" workshop and two solo performances.
- "Dynamic Anatomy" Workshops were taught during the '90s by Nancy Topf. She had just finished her successful 1998 workshop and was off to Geneva to teach—on Swiss Air Flight 111 which crashed off Nova Scotia. Her death was and is a terrible loss. However, her husband, musician Jon Gibson, and her students have continued to hold workshops based on her teachings and are overseeing the publication of the book she was writing at the time of her death.
- David Szepessy, world-renowned cellist, now teaches cello workshops.
- Workshops, such as Katie Brunault's Summer Dance Camp for Young Dancers, are directed by talented local artists.

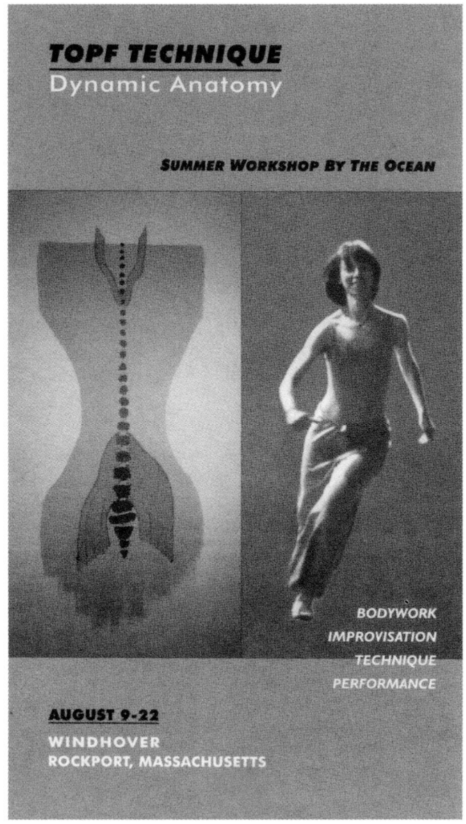

(above) Nancy Topf
(right) Risa Steinberg
(opposite) Lynn Simonson

Betty Jones as Desdemona in José Limón's

Beginning in 1986, Jazz Cabarets became an integral part of Windhover's performing season due to the talent and generosity of Joe Mulholland. Joe's contributions to the music programs and performances at Windhover go back to the camp days in the '70s when he was a virtual one-man music department.

Since then he has taught at several New England Colleges, including The New England Conservatory, Brown University, and Berklee College of Music, where he is currently an assistant professor. But Joe is not only a teacher, he's one of the finest jazz musicians in Boston, appearing regularly at the top jazz clubs in Boston and Cambridge with his group, The Joe Mulholland Sextet. He is a composer as well, who, to date, has released four CDs, which have received rave reviews from music critics. He is also the composer of several film scores, including *Last Stand at Little Big Horn*, an award winning documentary.

Joe has composed the music for many Windhover productions and dances, including both songs and music for *The Battle for Pigeon Cove Harbor, Dogtown Common,* and *Peer Gynt*. He has also accompanied jazz vocalist Didi Stewart every year since 1987 in our popular and always sold-out jazz cabaret evenings.

"We know the summer has arrived when Windhover's cabaret evenings begin." So said one of the hundreds of admirers of these special evenings. For fourteen years Didi Stewart and Joe Mulholland have played to sold-out houses at Windhover; in fact, they sell out months in advance. More than half of the audiences members return to hear them year after year.

In a review of their first season at Windhover in 1987, Susan Bulba said in *North Shore Magazine:*

> *"Mulholland's agility on the ivories was supplemented by dexterous self-accompaniment on the synthesizer, which made him a virtual one-man band. He combined a confident touch, a sure technique, and an endless creative imagination… a voice that can do anything…Stewart is a fine musician whose voice is so exactly on pitch that she has no difficulty with the dissonances of jazz…She can slide her voice like a trombone and bring it from the bass up to the highest ranges without a break. Stewart, formerly with the rock group "Girls' Night Out" and winner of Boston Magazine's Award for Best Jazz Vocalist, is a jazz singer the likes of which haven't been heard around these parts."*

Jazz vocalist Didi Stewart

Las Meninas Variations

Premiered in Boston at New England Life Hall in 1988
Choreography: Ina Hahn
Conception: Nelson Goodman
Music: David Alpher
Dancers: Carol Earle, Heidi Mason, Eden Mazer, Sallee Slagle, Beth Tragert
Costumes: Pamela Wise
"Las Meninas" was also performed at Endicott College in Beverly and at Windhover Performing Arts Center.

The idea for this dance came from a lecture and slide presentation entitled "Variations on Variation" by Dr. Nelson Goodman, philosophy professor emeritus of Harvard University. In 1957, Picasso painted forty-four variations of "Las Meninas" (The Maids of Honor), painted in 1656 by the Spanish court artist, Velasquez. To illustrate his lecture, Dr. Goodman made slides of twenty-two variations, which I then used in the dance. David Alpher composed the score as a musical analogy to the visual variations. I structured the dance, as well, in theme and variation form, paying particular attention to the nuances of the relationships between the princess and her entourage, as suggested by Picasso in his great series.

Picasso collapses the space; he depicts the Princess half in light, half in shadow, as the victim of preying and jealous maids of honor. It is his comment not only on the monarchy, which had been weakened by the 1950s when these were painted, but also on the repressive dictatorship of Franco, who still ruled, causing so much terror, grief, and mistrust among his people.

In May of 1999, I revisited Spain after an absence of thirty years. I had gone there in the '60s to study Flamenco with a great teacher in Seville and, of course, fell in love with Spain, its culture and people, its art, the poetry and plays of Lorca, and, most especially, its vibrant gypsy tradition of dance. My trip started in Madrid where, the very first day, I rushed to the Prado to again pay homage to "Las Meninas," Velasquez' masterpiece. It was more beautiful and alive than ever. I ended my trip in Barcelona, at the Picasso Museum, which felt like coming full circle. There, in three large rooms, hung all his variations of "Las Meninas," which I had only seen in reproductions before. I had not consciously planned the trip this way; it just happened that the ten days I spent in Spain in 1999 began and ended with and were magically colored by the very paintings I had so long ago attempted to capture in dance.

Excerpts of a letter from Eden Mazer, 14 years old, who danced the part of the Enfanta (The Princess):

> *"It's hard to put into words the feelings I have for you and Windhover. The past seven summers have created a person, inspired, imaginative, intuitive—three Is that shape the big I, me! Windhover has been a place to unfold dreams, reach to them, leap and twirl to them, dance to them. Thank you... I too will take the road less traveled by."*

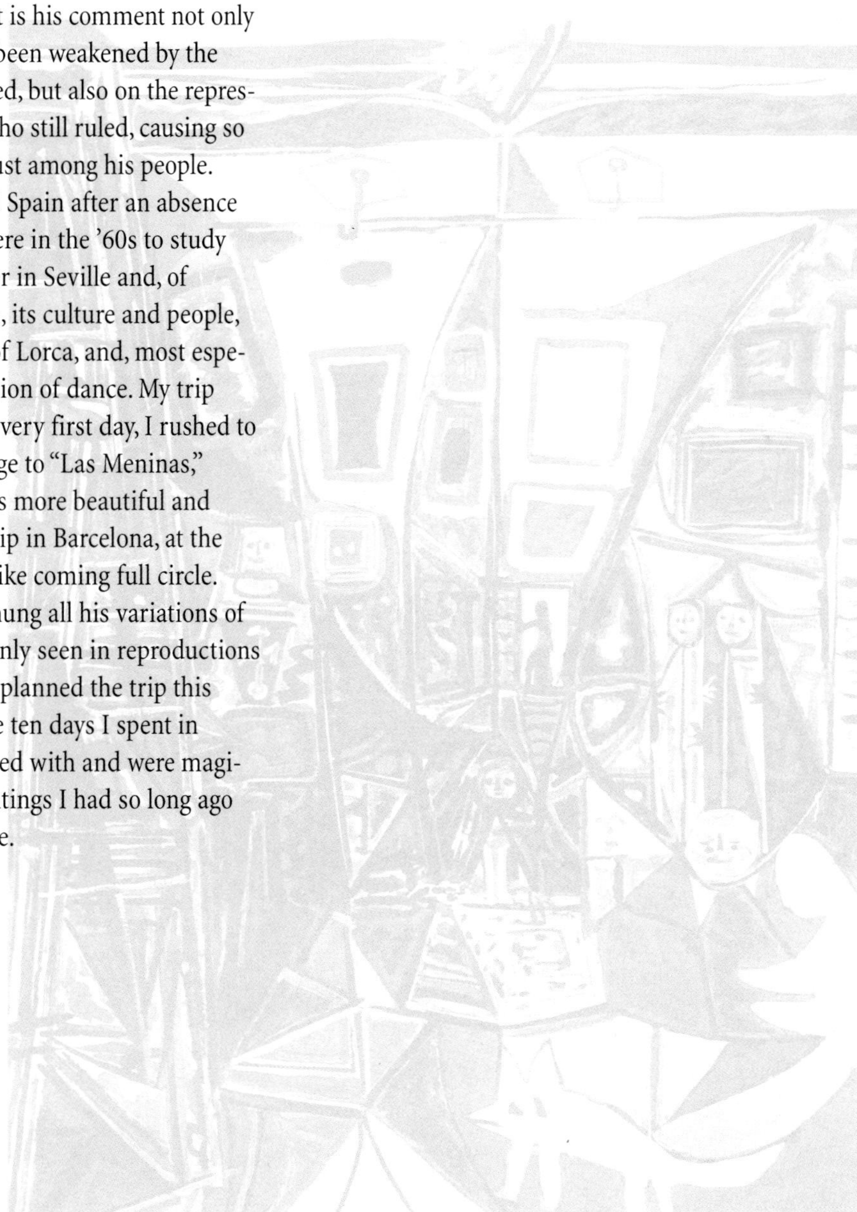

"For those of us who have a special feeling for our roots...probably the most memorable event was Windhover's outstanding production of Dogtown Common."

—Marshall Swan
President of the Sandy Bay Historical Society

"It is a testament to the perpetual energy and extensive creative imagination of Hahn, Angell, and Mulholland that Windhover's innovative performances are excitingly different from anything else being done on Cape Ann and beyond. Their concept is to fuse movement, music, and words into a theatrical experience that ignores the restrictive boundaries separating the arts. The goal is to strengthen the triangular bond between art, artist, and audience, creating a dynamic community-building experience.

The first and most successful project to emerge from the innovative collaboration was Dogtown Common, *a performance created around Percy MacKaye's early 20th century poem about life and spirituality in Cape Ann's first colonial settlement.*

Revived for the third straight year, the performance itself moves around outdoors taking complete advantage of the Cape Ann terrain, finally settling down at Windhover's performing space nestled at the edge of the woods.

"It's about community, so it's communal. The audience participates quite literally," explains Hahn. "The use of space is important because it's mythic. I think theater should be bigger than life. It should take us somewhere, change us somehow. It should be a very different experience from sitting in front of your television or going to the movies. It's a very living, present kind of energy."

"Straying from conventional theatrical presentation, Dogtown Common *supplies a double for each character in the form of a dancer. The dancers express in movement what the characters are feeling but not saying.*

Dogtown Common *is a dynamic, ambitious undertaking. It reaches beyond theater, beyond the moment, beyond the individuals involved...It is a gathering of communities. Through art a community of artists, a community of residents, and a community from Cape Ann's past are all brought together. Such a communion is designed to strengthen.* Dogtown Common *is an experience not to be missed."*

—Barry Madore
in North Shore Magazine, *July 1989*

"All in all it was a heady night with warm winds rushing about in the trees overhead and an intense struggle rushing about on the starlit acreage in front of us... For those lucky enough to be there, it certainly will be a night to remember."

—Rae Francoeur
Editor of North Shore Magazine, *July 1988*

Dogtown Common

An original adaptation of Percy MacKaye's epic poem
Design and Direction: George Angell
Choreography: Ina Hahn
Original Musical Score: Joe Mulholland
Opened at Windhover Performing Arts Center in 1987
Revived in 1988 and 1989, and again in 1999 by popular demand

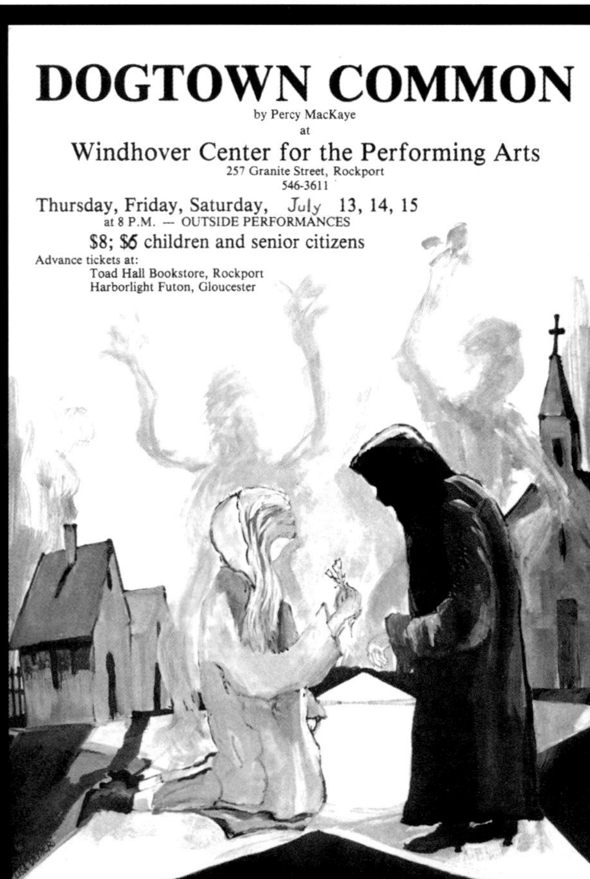

(above, left) Judy Rhines and her dancer spirit in Dogtown Common
(left) Herman Fritz as Peter Bray in Dogtown Common

"Set on their beautiful stage at 257 Granite St. Rockport, the Windhover production of Peer Gynt promises to be another extraordinary experience in text, movement, dance, and music such as only Windhover can provide. If you have never seen a production by this remarkable group, don't miss this one."

—Gloucester Times, *August 1988*

This letter ran in *The Boston Globe* on Tuesday, August 30, 1988:

FRESH, CREATIVE SPIRIT AT
CAPE ANN ARTS CENTER

On August 12, we discovered a Cape Ann jewel. We happened to attend the Windhover Center for the Performing Arts' adaptation of Henrik Ibsen's Peer Gynt.

Even though that was the last weekend of Rockport's little-known Windhover Center's 1988 summer season, we would like to share how we were moved by the quality, the adventuresomeness, and the fresh spirit of this production.

The delightfully creative interpretation of this play, about a man's life journey to find himself, effectively represents the aim of this performing arts group, which is the "fusion of dance and acting into a true theater of dramatic movement."

The performance was an ingenious blend of whimsy, metaphor, myth, humor, fantasy, and wisdom—all magnified by the lovely, woodsy outdoor setting.

Most striking to us were the talented performers, all multifaceted and energetic, who were obviously inspired by a loving sense of community which empowered each to shine in her or his own colorful way. It was clear to us, even as newcomers to the Windhover Series, that the people who created this theatrical experience gave their utmost. The high quality of the performance deserved a larger audience and wider recognition.

We believe that Windhover is an irreplaceable training ground for young people in the performing arts. It is also a gem for those of us who love good dance and theater. May Windhover become increasingly appreciated for its true brilliance by the larger artistic community of Cape Ann and New England."

—Teryl Lundquist, Cambridge
—Jeane Weikert, Rockport

Director George Angell's Note:

"Why Peer Gynt?. . . *Our aim is the fusion of dance and acting into a true theater of dramatic movement. By its very nature dance is an interpretive rather than a representational art form. Hence we wish to work with dramatic pieces that are not literally realistic but rather mythic and imagistic in their approach. We have no interest in pursuing realism; it is readily available to the public in television, film, and even other Cape Ann theaters.*

Written in Ibsen's youth, Peer Gynt is an abstract, unrealistic play based on folk mythology and fairytale. We were irresistibly attracted by the combination of beautiful verse, fairytale characters and allegorical thematic content to tackle this immense project."

Peer Gynt

An adaptation of Ibsen's delightful, fanciful masterpiece
Presented at Windhover in 1988
Direction and Design: George W. Angell
Choreography: Ina Hahn and Carol Earle
Original Musical Score: Joe Mulholland

Clockwise from top:
Cortney Strother as Peer Gynt
A celebratory dance
Planning another adventure

CHAPTER 13

The Windhover Dance Connection (1990–1995)

The Windhover Dance Connection, a company of dancers primarily from the North Shore, was founded in 1990. Our aim was twofold: to create and perform original works by North Shore choreographers and to bring to the public, especially young dancers, an awareness of the rich heritage of modern dance. The first objective was a result of my increased ties to the community and its dancers. I had begun to teach in the area again and I felt there was an abundance of talent here, but a lack of both performance opportunity and studio spaces for classes and rehearsals.

Fortunately, Windhover could provide the spaces both for learning and performance. It also provided local dancers with the opportunity to take classes, and to learn the repertoire of some of the pioneers of dance through intensive one- or two-week workshops taught by internationally-recognized artists.

The American dance movement in the twenties and thirties was one of the most fertile and groundbreaking of all the art movements in this century—equal to the revolutions in painting and music—yet not many people, including young dancers, have had access to the works of these pioneers. For these reasons, and because I had performed with many of these legendary choreographers whose works might otherwise be lost, I went to New York to study Labanotation—a notation system much like music's—in order to read and then reconstruct their dances. After a year, I received my

FRIDAY, JULY 25 at 8 P.M.

SATURDAY, JULY 26 at 8 P.M.

THE WINDHOVER DANCE CONNECTION PRESENTS:

The Windhover Dance Connection is a company of dancers dedicated to the performance of works by pioneer modern dance choregraphers. Through the reconstruction of their works — many of them masterpieces and all of them groundbreaking — this newly formed group hopes to bring to the public, and especially to young dancers, an awareness of the rich heritage of modern dance. The American dance movement in the twenties, thirties, and forties was one of the great revolutions in the arts in this century, yet not many people have seen, or dancers experienced the works of its pioneers.

It is true that much of their choreography is now irretrievably lost. Dance has always been a fleeting art — an art of the moment. But some of this early work has been recorded, through the reconstruction of pieces by dancers who performed them, and, as with Doris Humphrey, through the foresight of choreographers who encouraged the filming and notating of their work. Today choreographers are recognizing the obligation to preserve their works — through film, video and dance notation. Major ballets by Balanchine, Paul Taylor, Anthony Tudor, and Hanya Holm, among others, are being filmed and notated. Even Martha Graham, who feels her style is so personal it can only be personally transmitted, has consented to have her works filmed (many of them by Richard Winik, Board Member of Windhover and President of W.W. Films). With filmed records and a notated score, the repertoire of masters — past and present — is now increasingly available. It is from such sources as well as personal contact with the artists that the pieces on this program were reconstructed.

"No poet, no artist of any art, has his complete meaning alone. His significance, his appreciation is his appreciation of his relation to the dead poets and artists. And he is not likely to know what (work) is to be done unless he lives in what is not merely the present, but the present moment of the past, unless he is conscious, not of what is dead but of what is already living."

T.S. Eliot — Tradition and Individual Talent

Members of the Company:
Patricia Adams
Charles Brunault
Stephen Fladger
Jimmy Raye
Beth Ricker
Sally Slagle
Pamela Wise

Apprentices:
Michelle Cerino
Brian Feinenbaum
Anna Lane
Heidi Mason
Carrie Bredice

Artistic Advisor: Ina Hahn

WINDHOVER FOUNDATION AND DANCE NORTH ALLIANCE

present

A WEEKEND OF DANCE

by DANCERS AND CHOREOGRAPHERS OF THE NORTHSHORE

August 20, 21, 22 at 8 P.M.

on the outdoor stage at WINDHOVER
CENTER FOR THE PERFORMING ARTS
257 Granite St., Route 127, Rockport

Rain date for Saturday performance is Sunday, August 23 at 8 P.M.
In case of rain, Thursday and Friday performances will be held indoors.

Admission: $10 Children & Senior Citizens $6

Tickets may be purchased at: Toad Hall Bookstore in Rockport
The Bookstore in Gloucester
Casa de Moda in Beverly
Dancers Partner in Salem

For information and reservations, call **(508) 546-3611**

These performances are funded by grants from
New England Biolabs, The Rockport Arts Lottery and The Gloucester Arts Lottery.

An improvisation session

Ballet barre

certification from the Dance Notation Bureau and was ready and eager to try my wings.

My first opportunity came when The Boston Conservatory asked me to reconstruct and stage Doris Humphrey's masterpiece set to Bach's great *Passacaglia and Fugue in C Minor*. Because I had danced one of the solo parts at the American Dance Festival in 1951, I felt somewhat familiar with the dance. But the task was daunting, as there were twenty dancers in the piece and I hadn't a clue as to what they did…until I read the score and studied it over and over. It really worked! The work was performed; the response was positive. So began my mission.

Since then I have staged many works by Doris Humphrey, Helen Tamiris, and Charles Weidman, in colleges from Florida to New York State. The formation of The Dance Connection Company and Windhover's special role in producing and presenting it was the result of this interest and the desire to bring classic modern dances to the North Shore community.

> *"No poet, no artist of any art, has his complete meaning alone. His significance, his appreciation is his appreciation of the dead poets and artists. And he is not likely to know what work is to be done unless he lives in what is not merely the present, but the present moment of the past, unless he is conscious, not of what is dead but of what is already living."*
>
> —*T.S. Eliot*
> *Tradition and the Individual Talent*

Notation Score from "Water Study," choreographed by Doris Humphrey in 1928

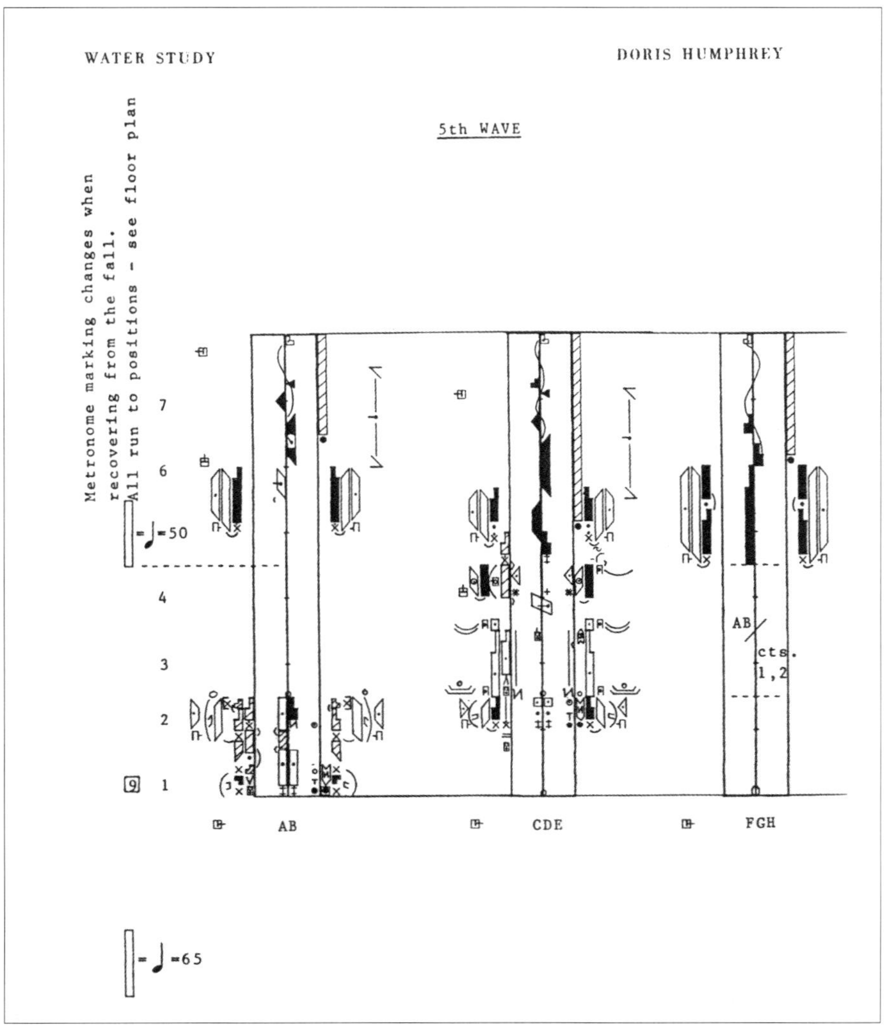

Kurt Weill Suite

Performed by dancers of the Windhover Dance Connection in 1991
Music and Lyrics: Kurt Weill
Choreography: Ina Hahn
Costumes: Pamela Wise
Dancers: Caroline Bredice, Pamela Wise, Sallee Slagle, Carol Earle, Charles Brunault, Marilda Castro

Clockwise from top left: Carol Earle, Sallee Slagle, Caroline Bredice. "If you've got a human heart, harden it into stone…"
Street scene: Marilda Castro and Charles Brunault
"Alabama Song" from Kurt Weill Suite

Clockwise from left:
"Je ne t'Aime Pas" with Carol Earle and Charles Brunault
"Speak Low" with Sallee Slagle and Charles Brunault
"Now you are a rich man..Now you can do what you want."

I heard Ute Lemper sing Kurt Weill's songs in concert and was immediately taken with her interpretation. Her voice was perfect for the cabaret style rendering of the songs, and her presence was electric. She was brazen, sassy, and moved like some feline creature. I felt she made a strong statement about the power of women. But what inspired me to create a dance suite was the irony expressed in the lyrics. Though written in the thirties, Weill's songs are as much a reflection of our times as his. I believe we live in an age of irony, and it was refreshing to hear that expressed in an art form.

Cycle

Music: Vivaldi Guitar Concerto
Choreography: Ina Hahn

Clockwise from top left:
Pamela Wise and Eden Mazer (1993)
Michaelangelo's Pieta
Carol Earle and Eden Mazer (1991)

In 1960, I had just returned from Rome where I had seen Michelangelo's "Pieta" tucked quietly away in a niche in St. Peters. No one else was there, so I had the luxury of standing in front of it for a long time, mesmerized. The image stayed with me long after. My mother had died the year before and my third daughter, Lauri, had been born that spring. My friend and collaborator, Erma Wheeler, gave me a recording of Vivaldi's guitar concerto. The dance—about a mother daughter relationship and the cycle of birth and death—came so easily and set so well to Vivaldi's concerto; it had its own life from the beginning.

I performed "Cycle" at Bradford College with one of my advanced students in 1961. Since then, the dance has undergone its own cycles as different couples have performed it over the past 35 years, in almost as many different venues. Its appeal has been widespread—a universal story of the cycle of birth and life and death, wherein the child becomes the mother and where the one who is nurtured becomes the one who gives sustenance, where the roles are reversed and death and birth become one.

This dance has become a metaphor for my life at Windhover, as I watch former students—my own daughters and another generation of committed and talented friends—begin to take over and I begin to rethink my roles as director, producer, teacher, choreographer, administrator, grant-writer, financial officer, cleaner, painter, chief cook, and bottle washer…!

Mari Jackman and Ina Hahn (1961)

CHAPTER 14

Doris Humphrey Centennial Celebration (1995)

At Windhover Performing Arts Center, July, 1995 and Fuller School, Gloucester, with the Cape Ann Symphony, October, 1995

"Doris Humphrey is an enduring part of the dance in America as granite under the soil is enduring. We can turn nowhere without finding her."
—John Martin
in The New York Times

As soon as I learned that 1995 would be the centennial year of Doris Humphrey's birth (1895-1958), with celebrations across the globe, I was determined to celebrate her on Cape Ann. What an opportunity to pay homage to the artist who had influenced me the most in my creative life. Fortunately, I found Joe Gifford, who had danced in her company in the forties and now lived in nearby Boston. He was as excited as I about bringing her work to the public. We chose "Shakers" because he was familiar with this dance and because it was such a pioneering and dramatic work. Joe had not only danced in the original production, but had staged it for her many times.

I was happy to also have the chance to re-stage "Water Study," another groundbreaking pioneering work, choreographed in 1928. It is one of the few dance pieces ever created that is performed entirely in silence—a group of 8 or 10 dancers with nothing but their breathing to keep them together. I knew it well, having staged it several times before—in Boston and Florida.

Joe Gifford

Finally, "Two Ecstatic Themes" was chosen because it had been a solo for Doris herself and gave insights into her theories of movement, especially the famous "fall and recovery" theory. The dance is about "falling" in love, literally. The first half comprises one long swoon, or fall; the second half, a struggle to regain balance, ending in a strong upright stance.

With these three classic Humphrey works on our program we felt confident that our celebration of her Centennial would do her justice. We were gratified that audiences came from every state in New England to see her work, that their reception was so overwhelmingly positive, and that the weather was beautiful for all performances, so that, despite huge crowds, we did not have to turn anyone away.

"Great as she (Humphrey) was as a dancer, she is even greater in the role of choreographer, ranking as one of the best, perhaps the very best, that America has produced."
—Walter Terry
dance critic of The Herald Tribune

"Shakers," premiered in 1931, has been called a living classic, "a dance of outward brilliance and inward grace." It is based on the means by which the Shaker sect believed they could literally shake off their sins. In Shaker worship, songs, tunes, and dances were inseparable forms expressing praise, joy, yearning, and union. In Shaker communities, the men and women were separated, and thus did not intermingle even in their religious rituals. So, too, in the dance, there is an imaginary line down the center dividing the sexes.

"The choreography is as austere, functional and beautiful as Shaker furniture, honoring the emotions rather than burlesquing them. Although Humphrey herself said most dances are too long and kept hers short, I wanted this one to go on."

—Elisabeth Clark
North Shore Magazine

Shakers

Choreography: Doris Humphrey (1931)
Direction: Joseph Gifford
Re-staging: Ina Hahn
Music: Traditional
Dancers: Charles Brunault, Lara Colabelli, Sandee Havunen, Bill Healy, Jamie Huggins (guest artist), Bonnie O'Leary, James Raye, Sallee Slagle, Pamela Wise

Clockwise from top left:
Joe Gifford rehearsing "Shakers"
The imaginary line between men and women
Sandee Havunen in "Shakers" rehearsal

"It's eight dancers and one breath."

—Boston Globe, *July 1995*

"Water Study is performed in silence—the dancer's breath sounds and the wind through the trees behind the stage providing the only accompaniment. Curved spines undulate slowly, but no musical beat sets the rhythm. The break, crash, and fall of waves are marked only by the dancers' collective breathing... Halfway through the piece I found myself breathing with them."

—*Elisabeth Clark*
North Shore Magazine

Charles Brunault in "Water Study"

Water Study

Choreography: Doris Humphrey (1928)
Re-staged from the Labanotation Score: Ina Hahn
Costumes: Pamela Wise
Dancers: Lara Colabelli, Caroline Fitzpatrick, Sandee Havunen, Bonnie O'Leary, Eden Mazer, Margaret Prindle, Sallee Slagle, Pamela Wise

"Water Study" performed on Windhover stage

Carol Earle

Two Ecstatic Themes

Choreography: Doris Humphrey (1931–1932)
Re-staging from the Labanotation Score: Ina Hahn
Dancer: Eden Mazer

This dance contains the first full exhibition of Humphrey's principle of fall and recovery, the alternate yielding to and resisting gravity that give the movement its spatial design. Also important are successions, movement impulses that travel through the body like the life force itself.

Carol Earle and Eden Mazer each performed this dance at Windhover. Carol's performances were in 1987; Eden's were in 1995 as part of the Doris Humphrey Centennial Celebration.

> *"The solo, exquisitely danced by Eden Mazer, is an expression of falling in love and struggling to retain balance, full of liquid swoons and the characteristic Humphrey suspension and fall."*
>
> —*Elisabeth Clark*
> North Shore Magazine, *July 20, 1995*

> *"Mazer was radiant, her performance sure and steady."*
>
> —*Diane Grant*
> The Boston Globe, *July 22, 1995*

"Passacaglia and Fugue in C Minor," first performed at Bennington College in 1938, has been called a masterpiece. Immediately after its performance it was recognized as a "grand, moving and brilliant composition." Composed for a large group of dancers—fourteen plus two soloists—the dance is, as Doris said, "an abstraction with dramatic overtones." The dancers move through the space, carving it and extending it in a "visual harmony and counterpoint" that corresponds to the architecture of Bach's music.

> *"As a dancer, Doris Humphrey is second to none. As a choreographer, she is first of all."*
>
> —*Margaret Lloyd*
> *dance critic,* Christian Science Monitor

In a review of Windhover Dancers in *North Shore Magazine*, Gail Lowe wrote:

> *"This performance was stunningly beautiful, a delight to both eye and ear, as the dancers dramatized the visual harmony and counterpoint corresponding to the architecture of Bach's music."*

Passacaglia and Fugue in C Minor

Choreography: Doris Humphrey (1938)
Re-staged from the Labanotation Score: Ina Hahn
Costumes: Pamela Wise
Dancers: Nancy Appel, Charles Brunault, Kate Brunault, Lara Colabelli, Caroline Fitzpatrick, Sandee Havunen, Bill Healy, Juliana McGovern, Bill Mclaughlin (guest artist), Bonnie O'Leary, Jimmy Raye, Sallee Slagle, Beth Tragert, Pamela Wise

Windhover dancers performing "Passacaglia" with The Cape Ann Symphony

Doris Humphrey in "Passacaglia"

CHAPTER 15

A Vision Realized (1997)

THE BATTLE FOR PIGEON COVE HARBOR

This original musical, which premiered at Windhover in August of 1997 and went on to play at the Gloucester Stage Company in October of that same year, was the culmination of all that Windhover stood for during its thirty-year history. The musical celebrated the **community** in every possible way; it affirmed the **inter-action of all the arts** and it was about preserving a **place** and its legacy. Moreover, it did so with zest and joy—through the arts of song, dance, and drama, the same powerful combination the Greek playwrights used to get their message heard. "The Battle" attracted large audiences—over one thousand people saw it at Windhover—and extra performances were scheduled. A fall season of ten shows was presented at Gloucester Stage Company and another thousand attended. Many others were turned away. There were standing ovations and the critics cheered...

This work truly resonated with its audiences.

"One of the best plays ever produced here, and the best musical by miles."

—Joe Garland
Author

Richard Earle and Ina Hahn with boat owners in Pigeon Cove Harbor

THE MESSAGE BEHIND "THE BATTLE"

From the moment in September of 1993 that I saw two fishermen standing at the entrance to Pigeon Cove Wharf with signs reading "Save the Wharf," I was hooked.

As a "Cove-er" for almost forty years I had walked down that wharf more times than I could count, treasuring it as a unique place—views from every vantage point, granite sea wall, shacks for gear, fishing boats coming and going—in short, a true working harbor where ordinary people could still earn a living. Small wonder that throughout the boat owners' year-long struggle to ensure public access to this harbor, I was totally committed to their cause.

That commitment grew even stronger as I got to know many of them—not at all the "rough guy" stereotypes some would have me believe. I found them to be intelligent, caring, and totally individual. During the long months of 1993-94 before their final victory I became more and more impressed with their measured response to all that was thrown at them, and their articulate, often poetic statements about what they were fighting for.

Their story stayed with me, haunted me, long after it was over. I wanted to tell about it, to celebrate it in the only way I knew how—through some kind of theatrical event using language, music, and dance. In the fall of 1996, I began a series of taped interviews with six key members of the Boat Owners Association who were leaders in that fight. Their recollections and language became the inspiration and outline for the script. Their individual stories created the characters.

I then asked Richard Earle and Joe Mulholland if they would collaborate with me. From then on it was as if the story had a life and spirit of its own. Richard wrote and re-wrote until a plausible script emerged. He worked intensively with Joe, who set lyrics to music, and in the space of a few months twelve songs and dance music appeared. We had a full-fledged musical on our hands! The energy spilled over to everyone involved—all volunteering time, energy and talent to this production. "It took a community," Jim Waddell said about the real Battle. So, also, has this re-creation.

Gordon Baird and Joe Mulholland rehearse "With Respect"

My hope is that this story has a life beyond this production, because its theme is so relevant today. It is an American story, if you will. Everywhere the common interest is threatened by the few, or, if not threatened, ignored. Whether it is the clear-cutting of national forests, the destruction of wetlands or the Everglades, over-fishing, over-grazing, or denying public access to the ocean, the issues are the same: private profit, in the name of "progress," versus public good.

Here, for a change, the small guy won. That victory should encourage common people everywhere to take heart—to fight for what they believe are their rights. And, even more, to educate the next generation never to take this wonderful, fragile planet for granted. We alone are responsible for it. We are earth's caretakers. Without it we cannot survive. That is the real message.

Directors Richard Earle and Ina Hahn

RICHARD EARLE
(Co-Writer, Lyricist, Director)

Richard Earle studied stage directing with Curt Canfield at Amherst College, where he was an English and American Studies major with a music minor. Following a two year stint as a Writer-Producer-Director at WBZ-TV in Boston, he was a Co-founder and Producer of the Carousel Theater in Framingham, Massachusetts, supervising 30 original productions of classic American musicals starring Ginger Rogers, Howard Keel, John Raitt, Gordon MacRae, Tony Perkins, Patrice Munsel, Cab Calloway, Dolores Gray, and many others. During this time, Earle discovered and gave first professional roles to Metropolitan Opera star Tatiana Troyanos and Tony Award-winner Donna McKechnie.

After moving to New York, Richard spent thirty years at various New York advertising agencies, most recently as Executive Vice President and Creative Director at Saatchi & Saatchi. During this time, he nourished his love of the Broadway Musical as a member of Lehman Engel's famed BMI Musical Theater Workshop, participating as a book writer, composer, and lyricist.

Richard has also collaborated as lyricist on various TV commercial, film, and stage scores with Top Ten songwriters Joe Brooks and Gershon Kingsley, Academy Award winner Fred Karlin, Sesame Street composer Joe Raposo, and West Side Story orchestrator and Boston Pops arranger Sid Ramin.

Now residing in Lanesville with his wife Pat, who was Stage Manager for the production of "The Battle for Pigeon Cover Harbor," Earle currently serves as advertising consultant to the Massachusetts Department of Public Health for their "Make Smoking History" anti-tobacco campaign.

The collaboration with Ina Hahn and Joe Mulholland on "The Battle" was an outgrowth of years of friendship and support for Windhover. Richard and Pat's daughter, Carol Earle, was both a dance student and faculty member at Windhover and danced principal roles with the Windhover Dancers.

Richard is also the author of the book *The Art of Cause Marketing*.

From an article in *North Shore Magazine:*

A ROCKPORT BATTLE IS SET TO MUSIC

"Even if "The Battle for Pigeon Cove Harbor" goes on to play at the Gloucester Stage Company, Music Theater, or Broadway (and why not?), it could never be as rousing, as delightful, as joyous as it was at Windhover Performing Arts Center in Rockport—a granite chip's toss from where the real-life battle was fought.

The musical, written by Ina Hahn and Richard Earle with music by Joe Mulholland, is about how a group of Rockport fishermen lost access to their boat moorings—and nearly their livelihoods—when developers took over the wharf from which the fishermen operated. It isn't exactly as cut and dried as good vs. evil. As one fisherman in the play said, it was more of a matter of "survival vs. profit"—a desperate situation.

Clearly the story's conflict made for great theater. And fishing, as the best-selling author of The Perfect Storm *Sebastian Junger discovered this summer, is fraught with a tension that compels masses of people.*

Earle said writing the play and lyrics was almost a spiritual experience—the work poured forth once he and Hahn were fortified with the research she had done. There are 10 songs—some such as "The Gear" and "Six Big Guys in a Little-Ass Boat" are laugh-out-loud funny, inspired and clever, regardless of how we proudly embrace this "local" creation.

Windhover is indeed the place to see this play. For one thing, the setting is exquisitely wild and beautiful. It's isolated and resembles a rocky old New England farm, the type most farmers abandoned a century ago, and not unlike the look and feel of overgrown Dogtown Common in the wilds of Gloucester.

The stage is outdoors, perched on granite and open to the elements. On the night we attended, the tops of the big trees rustled in a sea breeze. It was hot, in the high 80s at least, but the winds soothed and a huge vanilla-colored moon bored through a flurry of fast-moving, high clouds.

The sold-out crowd was filled with friends and acquaintances from Cape Ann; the writers were there; even the actors were familiar faces to most

OUR TOWN

'Battle' belongs on the Broadway stage

Boston Sunday Globe

SEPTEMBER 21, 1997

NORTH WEEKLY

Theater production pays tribute to fight waged by fishermen

By John Laidler
GLOBE CORRESPONDENT

ROCKPORT – When fishermen waged a successful battle to preserve public access to one of the town's scenic coves in 1993-94, local theater owner Ina Hahn was so moved by their struggle that she decided to try to find a way to recreate it on stage.

"It's a story about not looking elsewhere for your heroes, but right in your back yard, in your community," said Hahn, who was a strong supporter of the fishermen from the beginning of their battle against a planned marina in Pigeon Cove harbor.

Her inspiration led Hahn to collaborate with Richard Earle and others in presenting "The Battle for Pigeon Cove Harbor," a lively musical that played for two weeks last month at Hahn's outdoor Windhover Center for the Performing Arts.

The participants in the real-life drama took inspiration from the theater presentation. Since opening night, the fishermen, many of whom rarely take in a theater event, have been raving about the production, saying it faithfully recreates both the details and the intense emotions of their battle.

"We are jubilant about this," said Peter Prybot, a lobsterman who was a spokesman for the 35 fishermen and other boatowners involved in the marina battle.

"We thoroughly enjoy this, because we've gone through it. We can feel the whole thing. It's so emotional. It's deep down inside of us, and for some of us, it almost brought us to tears," said Prybot, who saw the show three times.

"I don't think there's a person on our side of the fence who didn't love it. We felt it accurately depicted the way we felt during the battle," said Bob Morris, a lobstermen who went to the show every night.

The response by fishermen has helped draw attention to "The Battle of Pigeon Cove Harbor" and to extend its life. The show is set to be performed again at the Gloucester Stage Company Oct. 29-31, Nov. 1-2 and Nov. 5-9.

The saga that forms the basis of the show began in the summer of 1993, when Craig Hillier, a former fisherman, leased the Pigeon Cove waterfront, including the public wharf traditionally used by fishermen, from its owners. Hillier and a group of investors made plans to build a large marina.

Hillier soon stirred the wrath of fishermen and other boatowners

PLAY, Page 7

Ina Hahn with boat owners Bob Morris and Fred Hillier

of us. We had lived through this struggle together and now it had come back to us: assessed, given a perspective, put to music and dance. Art, from the community and to the community, is the best kind of gift.

And it was art……

The fishermen/actors who show us this conflict should go to Broadway along with the play. Not all of them can project like a Pavarotti, but they have remarkable spirit and energy. Gordon Baird, known to many as the man who sails every day regardless of the weather, charmed everybody with his vibrant portrayal and his assertive singing talent. And the testy, unpredictable Coot (Herman Fritz) definitely endears over time. His raucous song "I'm Cool" could serve as a psychologist's study in denial.

I wouldn't have thought this conflict would lend itself to humor, but the play is rife with genuine laughs. The rap song about how to fish is full of technical detail yet presented with delicious confidence and expertise. When shuttling to their moors in a tiny skiff, the six fishermen clown despite the mounting severity of their crisis. A favorite line: "If a man says something in a forest and there's no woman around, is he still wrong?"

Yet when the pictures of Rockport's many real-life Pigeon Cove fishermen are projected onto a backdrop during the closing song, we are restored to a sober reality. Yes, these are tough, hard-working men, but the pictures remind us that it's impossible to stereotype a group of men who happen to share a common profession. One day they are fishing, the next they are squeezed by changing times. Their crisis is our crisis.

We're told the accolades are pouring in. Accolades are not enough. This play deserves a life beyond Windhover and such discussions, we hear, are going on. If Jon Kimbell happens to be listening, "The Battle for Pigeon Cove Harbor" would be perfect for North Shore Music Theater…for starters."

—Rae Francoeur
North Shore Magazine

The Battle For Pigeon Cove Harbor

Book: Ina Hahn and Richard Earle
Music: Joe Mulholland
Lyrics: Richard Earle
Additional Lyrics: Ina Hahn

Clockwise from top left:
Sandee Havunen in "Dance of the Fisherman's Wife"
Herman Fritz, as Coot, rehearses "I'm Cool"
The cast in "Send Them a Message"

CHAPTER 16

Dogtown Revisited (1999)

For many people, Dogtown, a large area of forest, rocky terrain, and glacial boulders in the center of Cape Ann, is a place to bike, hike, ride horses, watch birds, and pick blueberries. It is also an area with a rich history that has inspired painters and poets. Established in the 18th century as a colonial farming village, it was abandoned because of difficulty working the land and became inhabited by social outcasts, wild dogs, and, according to some, witches. In 1921, Percy MacKaye wrote an epic poem, "Dogtown Common," about the real-life inhabitants of the area and the lore that surrounds them…

Ten years after the last 1989 staging of *Dogtown Common,* I felt it was time to reaffirm this celebration of place. So much had happened in the last decade to weaken the sense of place and community. What has been called "urban sprawl" had begun to affect Cape Ann as well. This place which we thought would stay so isolated from the rest of the bustling world was now being discovered and changes were occurring , including the development of formerly unspoiled woodlands, and the increased private claims on public rights of way. A booming economy and the means to dig, dredge, and cut into hitherto inaccessible granite outcroppings, plus a lack of preparedness for the onslaught of developers, made us easy targets. Our community had no updated zoning regulations or plans to preserve the open spaces which we had taken for granted for so long: public rights of way by the ocean, woodlands where our children could play, harbors to which we still had access, quarries in which we freely swam. We were now increasingly confronted with "private" and "no trespassing" signs, gates, and, often, hostility.

Windhover play promises to be magical

The narrators: Julia Mueller, Susan Souza, and Mike Carter

Alison Landoni as Judy Rhines and Eden Mazer as her spirit

We had inherited a place still wild and free, a playground and paradise, because those who were here before us kept it that way. They farmed or quarried or fished, but they kept quarries, fields, pastures, or harbors open to all. They were workers, bound to the land or the sea, with love and respect for the place and little thought of selling any of it for a profit. Now as a new generation inherits the land, what will happen to it?

When I heard talk of building a road through Dogtown, a special kind of place full of history and lore, woods and paths, swamps, boulders as tall as houses, and blueberries as big as grapes, I felt it was time to bring back *Dogtown Common* as an education for our newer citizens, for young people who know so little of their heritage, and as a reminder to all of us.

WINDHOVER'S DOGTOWN COMMON
CASTS ITS SPELL

"In the moment, this place is more magical than any other place and these words (of Percy MacKaye's) more captivating than any other words and these spirits are more enchanting than any other spirits."

—Gail Mountain
The Gloucester Daily Times, *August 27, 1999*

"It was a very compelling evening of theater, and the choreography a major part of the evening's strong impact."

—Victor Rosenbaum
Longy School of Music

"We enjoyed a superlative evening at Dogtown Common… The entire evening was mystical."
—Kenneth Wile MD, Rockport

"These are our stories, our New England stories, about our place, our ocean, our land."

—Donald Oliver
Graduate School of Education, Harvard University

(opposite) Clockwise from top left:
Dance Spirits Eden Mazer and Al Turner
Jape Payette as John Wharf and Al Turner as his spirit
The cast of Dogtown Common
Rick Doucette as Peter Bray leads the party to the witch's house

Dogtown Common

"Dogtown Common," A Verse Drama by Percy MacKaye
Presented at Windhover, August 1999
Direction: Nan Webber
Original music and sound design: Joe Mulholland
Choreography: Ina Hahn

Our mission remains the same. Windhover must always provide the highest quality instruction and performances in the arts, encourage original works in dance/theater/music, and include the community in all aspects of its programs. A task force consisting of Board members and others who care about Windhover's survival has been created. Its goal is to increase the number of workshops, classes, and performances we offer by extending our summer season and by re-building our rear studio so that it becomes a viable theater. As a result, we will be able schedule events and additional performances with the assurance they will not be rained out. We will always use the outdoor stage and garden as the primary performance area, but we will have a back-up space right next to it—the best of both worlds!

Plans have been drawn up by architect and planner Prataap Patrose, who has volunteered his expertise. Now the goals are to raise funds and donations of materials and labor for this exciting enterprise.

Another primary goal is to increase public awareness of this special place. How many times people have said, "I saw the sign but I just saw a field and didn't know where to go" or "I pass it all the time but don't know much about it." This book is an attempt at filling that gap.

Before embarking on this project—a book about Windhover—I had to ask myself, "Why? What was my goal in writing this book? To whom would it be addressed? What purpose would it serve?"

The answer came during one of my many walks with my three-year-old granddaughter. She directed me, as we set out on the path through the woods, "You be the wolf, grandma, and I will be the baby bear." Of course, I complied and, under her prompting and guidance, I was transformed into a nasty, mean wolf and she into the beleaguered baby. The story grew, became embellished with movement, voice changes, and songs, until we had exhausted all possibilities and she was finally triumphant. Further along on the walk, I was the Prince and she Rapunzel, standing a-top a granite wall as I urged her to let her hair down and run away with me. In all, we enacted five different stories on that mile-and-a-half walk, each taking place in and utilizing a unique space along the way: woods, walls, rocks, road. I realized that this is natural to us, to imagine and create. And that is exactly what Windhover is—a place for the creation and performance of dance and music and theater events.

I also realized that while we enacted these dramas my granddaughter would never become cranky or difficult, never complain she was tired. Nor did I. On the contrary, our theater energized us both as we continually moved back and forth from the reality of the natural world to the world of fantasy. It appears that we human beings need both—indeed, that we have survived as a species because we excel in both the sciences of the earth and the worlds of possibilities opened up through the imagination.

What could be closer to the dialogue between matter and spirit than the art of dance, rooted as it is in the physical body, yet somehow transcending it. As a dancer I learned much about gravity—when to give in to gravity, when to play with it, when to challenge it. I learned the hard facts of anatomy and how to guard against or deal with injuries. I learned when to focus on whether the arm was curved or straight and when to imagine I was a witch, a siren, or a tree. "Either the toe is pointed or it is not," Martha Graham admonished her students. But then, she would also say, "The spiral is a coil and the release is a strike; hiss when you move through it, snarl as you retreat."

Our society has too few places like Windhover, places where people can be affirmed in what I believe is the most human of all attributes—that of imagination. We are strong on goods, the economy, technology, and information, but woefully weak in acknowledging the creative, imaginative side of ourselves.

The path has not been easy. It has been rough, rocky, full of difficult twists and turns. My husband, planner and builder of Windhover, died just seven years after we opened the camp; a beloved daughter died ten years later. And the financial burdens of maintaining the place are ever-present. I am, as they say, land rich and cash poor. But balancing the ledger have been countless young students whose lives Windhover has transformed, thousands of audience members whose lives it has enriched. I, too, am the beneficiary of a rich 32 years. I never cease to be inspired by the creativity and energy of the artists who have worked and performed at Windhover, or by my connection to a wonderful and diverse community of citizens: dancers, writers, actors, musicians, artists, fishermen, builders, volunteers—whose issues and interests continually inform my own.

And I never cease to marvel at the incomparable beauty of this paradise, Cape Ann.

The word "magic" is used by so many to describe what they feel here. "I was transformed by the play and by the setting"... "some kind of magic came over me." Indefinable, but felt in every corner of garden, of field, of studio is an energy shouting, "I'll build you a dance space!" Little did I imagine then that such energy would transform not just the place, but all whom it touched, including me.

My thanks to my daughters and best friends, Lisa and Lauri, without whose support, encouragement, and faith I simply could not have continued. Thanks to Richard "Dick" Winik for his belief that I can do whatever I dream I can do, and whose humor has sustained me through thick and thin.

...To my brothers, Arthur (Buddy) and Martin (Marty), who have supported my dreams ever since childhood.

...To Peter Prybot, fisherman/photographer, for his photos of "The Battle for Pigeon Cove Harbor," Pigeon Cove, and others.

...To Cheryl Mazer, for proof reading this book, and for being ready to assist in any task assigned—for the past fifteen years.

...To Sandee Havunen, for scanning all the photos, and for her superb dance artistry.

...To Joyce Bruce for the beautiful web page at www.windhover.org.

...To Doris and Stan Patey for volunteering their time and expertise to oversee the publishing of this book, and to Kristna Evans for her editing.

...To all who assisted in the creation of "The Battle for Pigeon Cover Harbor" and to director, Nan Webber, and her group of actors and actresses of Theater in the Pines, for bringing "Dogtown" to life again.

Thanks to New England Biolabs, the Bruce J. Anderson Foundation, and Robert Amory for their generous support of our programs for nearly a decade; to the Massachusetts Cultural Council; to the members of the Gloucester Cultural Council, whose support of the arts in this community is both informed and invaluable; to Toad Hall Bookstore and The Bookstore in Gloucester for handling our ticket sales during their busiest months; to the members of Windhover's Board, and the Task Force, a group of friends and artists who are planning for Windhover's future.

...To Pamela Wise, Carol Earle Burnham, Trish Walker, and Kristen Ledson for all they have contributed to the dance programs at Windhover for over two decades, and for the Windhover Dance Retrospective, *Moving Forward, Looking Back.* And to Didi Stewart, for over a decade of memorable jazz cabarets.

...To all the people who have contributed, volunteered, or worked here and left their imprint in every nook and cranny of the place—dancers, students, actors, actresses, teachers, directors, choreographers, composers, singers, painters, carpenters, fishermen, writers, friends, audiences...so many.

...And to the spirits of those who bloom each spring with the rhododendron in the garden—my parents; my husband, Herb; my daughter, Pamela. I thank you all.

I love all beauteous things
I seek and adore them
God hath no better praise
And man, in his hasty days,
Is honored for them.
I, too, will something make,
And joy in the making,
Though tomorrow it seem,
Like the empty words of a dream,
Remembered on waking.

—Robert Bridges

CARSON

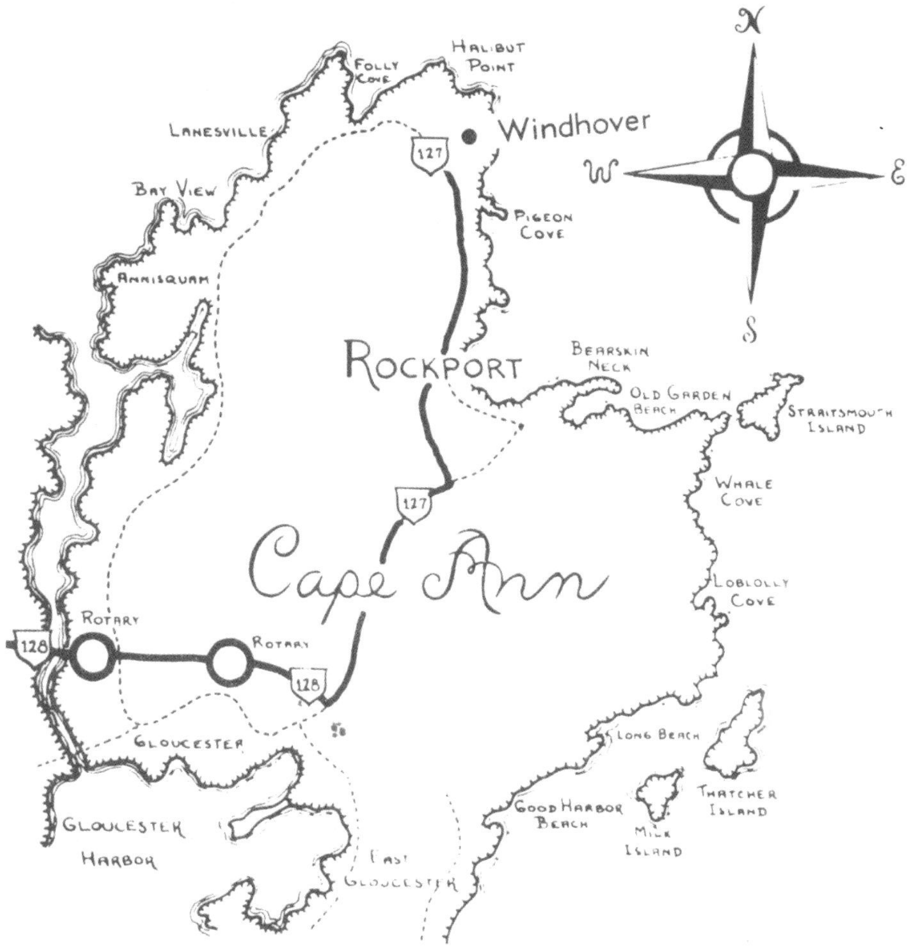
N
E
S
W
Halibut Point
Folly Cove
Windhover
Lanesville
127
Bay View
Pigeon Cove
Annisquam
Rockport
Bearskin Neck
Old Garden Beach
Straitsmouth Island
127
Whale Cove
Cape Ann
Loblolly Cove
Rotary
128
Rotary
128
Gloucester
Long Beach
Thatcher Island
Good Harbor Beach
Milk Island
Gloucester Harbor
East Gloucester